PRAISE FOR
THE GAINSHARING REVOLUTION

"Implementing gainsharing has been the single best thing we've ever done for our company."

Gary Hicks,
General Manager, and Steve Hicks, President,
Dongan Electric Manufacturing Company

"I'll tell anyone who asks me about our performance improvements from gainsharing that it's been just breathtaking!"

Jim Fitch,
President, Fitch Metal Solutions

"I was skeptical at first. But, I must admit, our performance improvements with gainsharing have convinced me."

Dave Maggart,
Information Systems Manager, Meyer Stamping

"I'm making more money now than ever, and I'm paying my people more." (One year after implementing gainsharing.)

Earl Chupp,
President, Woodenware USA

"Profit driver gainsharing made our year financially. It basically puts a new management culture into your business."

Bill Bugg,
President, Creation Windows

"I can't get over how people care about things [after implementing gainsharing] that they never cared about before."

Jody Fledderman,
President, Batesville Tool & Die

"Gainsharing has helped us understand our company better. It makes us pay attention to and take action on the things we need to do to be successful."

Chip Giardina,
Controller, Peerless Saw

"Profit driver gainsharing has given us a new level of visibility and accountability to things that we just lived with in the past. We are doing a better job of questioning and correcting now."

Russ Davies,
Operations Manager, Hasbro

"This gainsharing, it's on our people's minds 110%. If you talk with them, it's going to come up. They talk about it all the time. It's why they're motivated. It's why they bust their tails."

Stanton Lane,
Logistics Manger, Industrial Hardfacing

"Gainsharing has taken us to a new level of productivity."

Rodney Phipps,
Chief Financial Officer, Pentaflex

"The things profit driver gainsharing has shown us about our business and how to run it have been really helpful."

David Amatangelo,
President, Amatech

"This [profit driver gainsharing] is the best thing I've seen so far as a tool to help us beat our plan and get us to where we need to be."

Tim Mathis,
Manufacturing Manager, PPG

"Profit driver gainsharing, it's doing what it's supposed to be doing."

Bob Meyer,
Controller, Ripon Printers

"Profit driver gainsharing is forcing us into an organized management structure."

Wayne Bent,
General Manager, Available Plastics

"Gainsharing is the incentive to get your employees involved in your business. You have to be willing to give back to your employees to be successful—that is the key—it gives you a means of giving back."

Rick Craft,
Production Manager, Meyer Stamping

"I think the gainsharing concept is the greatest management tool that I have run into in my years of doing business very honestly. I like it and think it's the greatest thing since sliced bread in terms of trying to get everyone in your business involved in the business. And what I love about this program particularly is just the complete scope that it covers. There isn't a facet of our business that we don't somehow talk about periodically. I can't think of a better tool where you get everyone focused on your business."

Bob Sibilsky,
General Manager, Compak/Webcor

"The relationship between paying gainsharing bonuses and increased profits is perfect."

Dirk Benthien,
VP Administration & Finance, Wacker Chemical Company

"Gainsharing has put peoples' minds on track with what it is that we are all about, and that is getting quality products to the customers when the customers want them, understanding what throughput is, etc. With gainsharing, if we concentrate on throughput, it will enhance the peoples' pocketbooks as well as the company's pocketbooks."

Edmund S. Mende,
Chief Financial Officer, Century LLC

"Gainsharing has opened peoples' minds to what running the business is all about. Period. Its great! It's really concentrated our employees on increasing throughput, which is what it's all about."

Jim Black,
Plant Manager, Century Sun Metal Treating

"Gainsharing has taught us the meaning of teamwork."

Michelle Oldford,
Production Manager, Clips & Clamps Industries

"We have the ability to earn extra money through gainsharing. It's exciting!"

Barbara Carpenter,
Director of Human Resources, Dongan Electric

"Gainsharing has been a great problem-definition tool for SPM. It allows you to get things going faster. Overall, it has been a great help."

Dick Brannan,
Director of Operations, Special Products & Manufacturing

"Gainsharing has made our jobs easier and made us more of a team."

Steve Michaels,
Production Manager, Accudyn

"People are paying attention to things that they have never paid attention to before, all the way up and down the organizational chart."

Of all the things we have done, try to put in procedures, etc., nothing has had such a positive impact as what we have done with gainsharing."

John Shulton,
HR Manager, Berman Printing

"Of all the things we have done, try to put in procedures, etc., nothing has had such a positive impact as what we have done with gainsharing."

Kermit Engh,
President, Fashion Cleaners

"Gainsharing has helped us focus on making our shipments on time by getting everyone to pull together. We are presently anticipating an increase in our volume, and it has helped us get production, maintenance, tooling, and management all on the same page to be sure that things get done when they need to. We don't have the luxury of being able to postpone the jobs because another job will be scheduled to run later. Since we began gainsharing, our productivity has improved more than 20% and our scrap has also gone down about 20%. Gainsharing has really put a focus on our quality efforts lately, making us sure that everything we ship out of here has zero defects. When you first hear about gainsharing, it can sound too good to be true. But when you get everyone focused on improving throughput and eliminating the barriers, you can't help but be successful with it."

Timothy Fry,
Controller, Meyer Stamping

THE

GAINSHARING

REVOLUTION

Six Steps to Driving Motivation, Productivity, and Profits In Any Company

CHARLES DEBETTIGNIES, PH.D.

MOTIVATION PRESS

Want to Find Out More About Motivating Employees and Tying Pay to Performance?

We have a variety of options to learn more,
and many of them are **FREE**.

We update our offerings regularly.
To find the latest options, please visit the link below:

Gainsharing.com/nextsteps

CONTENTS

"He will win whose army is animated by the same spirit throughout all its ranks."

SUN TZU

INTRODUCTION

COMPANIES HAVE TROUBLE motivating their employees. But the trouble is caused by decisions they've made and the way employees are rewarded.

Companies have caused this problem. And they can solve it. This book will show you how.

Gainsharing has always attracted elite companies looking for a competitive edge, wanting to take performance to the next level and reward employees for performance.

You're reading this book because you're excited about your business and want everyone in your company to have the zest and excitement for challenge and achievement that you have.

As a successful businessperson, you've worked hard to bring your company to its current level of success. But you know your company needs to do better, and continuing to do things the same way isn't going to get your company the improved performance you want and need.

This book will show you how to focus everyone in your business on the factors that drive the bottom line. It will show you how to have a common message that provides a big-picture goal and answers the employee question, "What do I need to do today to earn a bonus?" What's more, it will show you how to take the complexity of your business and make it simple.

Like many other companies, you're probably experiencing some of the following problems and difficulties:

- **You want pay-for-performance benefits.**
  You're tired of giving raises without people having skin in the game. You want to implement some kind of pay-for-performance or bonus system. And you want annual raises to be reduced or go away, but you aren't sure how to make it work for your company.

  Employees expect pay increases for doing the same work. You even see some employees just putting in minimal effort and expecting pay increases.

  You know incentives work. You see other companies have implemented them successfully. But you don't know a solid way to motivate your employees and tie their pay to results.

- **You know year-end bonuses don't motivate employees.**
  You find year-end bonuses to be a bit meaningless because they're detached from daily operations. You don't have faith that your annual bonus arrangement does any good at all as a motivating tool.

  Plus, you're concerned your annual bonus could put you in a situation where people are expecting money, but then you have to tell them the numbers didn't work out and they won't get a bonus.

  But you know you need to incentivize performance or do something different because you don't want your current, unacceptable performance to remain the same.

- **You're in a job-shop environment.**
  You don't make the same thing over and over (repetitive work), so you don't understand how a bonus or pay-for-performance systems could work for you.

  You understand how a bonus system could be created where people do the same thing over and over. But you don't know how to put a bonus system together where the work isn't repetitive.

  The job-shop environment is quite common, though, and incentives work for other companies. So there must be a way to make it work for a job shop. But how?

SOLVING THESE PROBLEMS

This book reveals the secret code, the must-have elements to motivate employees and drive company performance, getting all employees on the same page, pulling in the same direction.

It's based on what has been proven to work in the real world and was developed through application at thousands of companies.

This book will show you how to reward employees for driving the profit and loss (P&L) items that drive profits. This creates a win-win situation where people can get bonuses for improvements in the bottom line.

This way, everyone's on the same page, driving the same success.

This shows employees how to make more money by driving company performance. It spells out the performance needed, gives them real-time feedback, and ties their bonuses to results, not effort.

This book will show you how to have potential bonuses throughout the year, typically on a monthly basis, not just a year-end bonus. This reduces the delay between performance and bonuses, and increases the motivational impact.

The six-step process outlined in this book shows businesses how to: 1) clarify the results and performance needed for employees to get their bonuses, 2) give them feedback to make adjustments along the way, and 3) give them a checklist that spells out what they need to do to get the bonuses they want.

This connects employees' pay to day-to-day operations. It turns their efforts to get a bonus into a game they're playing on a daily basis. This is a must-have for driving motivation and connecting people to their rewards.

The book you are reading will also show how to have a pay-for-performance system in a job-shop environment, where a company isn't making the same products over and over.

It's common for people to understand how piecework-type measures and incentives can be put together where the work is repetitive. But they don't understand how measures and rewards can be put in place where the work isn't repetitive, where there's great variability in the product mix, and where profit margins vary tremendously from job to job.

Measurement and reward systems can be put together for all kinds of companies, including a job-shop environment, and this book will show you how.

The ideas and techniques in this book are proven ideas. They've been developed during more than twenty years of study and hands-on work, testing and refining ideas in actual practice.

This book will show you the essential pieces to create an effective gainsharing pay-for-performance system. Each of the must-have pieces also adds to the momentum and effectiveness of the other pieces. "One hand washes the other," as the saying goes.

Once you have this system in place and your motivation problem is solved, it will stay solved. While you are solving problems, your competitors will still have this rock in their shoe that stymies motivation in their shop.

WHERE DID THE FIRE START?

My entire career has been focused on developing, implementing, and making companies successful by using gainsharing. It all started very early in my life.

I went to a grade school just a couple blocks away from the Indianapolis 500 Speedway. The school was so close to the track that we could hear the roar of cars in our classroom.

Each May, our city was flooded with people from all over the world who are absolutely committed to being the best they can possibly be, to achieving the highest performance possible.

For these IndyCar drivers, when they are in their car, they really feel alive. Everything else, for them, is just waiting. Race car drivers love what they do so much, they are so passionate about winning that they're willing to die in the process because it's part of who they are at their core.

Their devotion to excellence and high performance had a huge impact on me.

They would happily do anything and everything possible to achieve the best performance on race day. Good enough was not in their playbook.

It's well known among racing enthusiasts that crews test endless combinations of suspension, tires, and chassis arrangements, and they stay up all night disassembling and reassembling the car to make sure everything is the best it can possibly be.

With this level of commitment to excellence in mind, it was clear to me that some people at companies were excited about their work and woke up in the morning eager to tear into the challenge of the day. Other people were just waiting for Friday.

When I went off to college, I began to research how companies could be full of people excited about their work and devoted to being the best they could possibly be.

How could we create or remake high-performance companies like these IndyCar teams? Companies like that exist, so we know it's possible. But how does that happen? And how can we make it happen more?

I went on to graduate school to get a doctorate in industrial and organizational psychology and was introduced to gainsharing by a professor who allowed me to work with him on a gainsharing project. When I saw firsthand the exciting improvements in the gainsharing client's operations, I knew I had found what I was looking for.

His gainsharing project was at a steel fabrication plant. Productivity and scrap had improved, throughput had increased, and the shifts were leaving tape-recorded messages for the incoming shifts to improve communication. The employees were excited, motivated, and receiving bonuses.

After earning a PhD in my field, I went out into the workplace and began working full-time designing, implementing, and making companies successful with gainsharing.

After more than twenty years of hands-on implementation of gainsharing systems, I developed the six-step model presented in this book. It is the product of finding through trial and error what works and what doesn't work, and determining the essential elements for long-term success.

PROVEN RECORD

Gainsharing now has a proven record of improving productivity, lowering costs, and improving profits.

It works because it focuses everyone on the fundamentals that drive business success. Therefore, it never loses its effectiveness or validity.

Gainsharing has been successful in all kinds of companies: service, manufacturing, union, nonunion, large, and small, and I've been involved in it all.

There are three factors I'm looking for when a company is interested in implementing gainsharing:

- Is there healthy sales demand for the products they produce or services they provide?
- Do they have a management team that will look at the facts and data and make decisions based on those? They can't just continuously talk about their problems and not take action to address them.
- Will their equipment fail them? You can't win the Indianapolis 500 if your car is in the pits half of the time.

If a company has all three of these prerequisites, I fully expect to have at least a 5% improvement in productivity in the first year after implementation of gainsharing.

Much greater productivity gains are possible, and the gains typically continue to increase in future years.

MY CLIENTS SPEAK

In the process of preparing to write this book, I interviewed several of my clients who have implemented gainsharing. They were kind enough to provide their side of various elements of the gainsharing equation. I recorded these interviews and had them transcribed. Many of their thoughts are faithfully shared here for your benefit, in both short and extended passages. I thank all of them for their contributions to the understanding of gainsharing.

EXAMPLES OF GAINSHARING SUCCESSES

Thousands of companies have successfully integrated gainsharing into their company's practices. They can be found in disparate places. I have many examples among my own clients in the United States. Here are several:

- **Structural steel fabrication company**
  80 employees, mid-South
  Before implementing gainsharing, labor was 31.48% of sales costs. In the twelve months after gainsharing, labor was 22.89%. This is a 27.3% productivity improvement.
  Profits went from -7.93% of sales before gainsharing to 6.68% of sales in the twelve months after implementing gainsharing.

- **Glass manufacturer**
  150 employees, Midwest
  Achieved a 7.24% productivity improvement in the six months after implementing gainsharing

- **Plastic injection molding**
  260 employees, northern Midwest
  First-year labor productivity improved 15.9%, plus employee bonuses increased 80% compared to the previous year.

- **Metal fabrication**
  200 employees, mid-South
  Productivity improved 11.55% over a five-year period. Profits improved 323%.

- **Clothing design and manufacturing**
  150 employees, Midwest
  Twelve months after implementing gainsharing, direct labor productivity had increased by 15.4%. Annual profit increased

78%, even though sales had declined 7.6%. This was possible through better control of labor costs during lower sales months, combined with improved productivity overall.

- **Metal finishing**
  385 employees, northern Midwest
  Achieved 6.5% productivity improvement in the first year with gainsharing

- **Electrical equipment manufacturer**
  80 employees, Midwest
  Achieved 18.5% productivity improvement and has paid over $2.2 million in bonuses since implementing gainsharing

- **Plastic injection molding**
  150 employees, Midwest
  6.4% productivity improvement achieved in the first year after implementing gainsharing

- **Food manufacturer**
  350 employees, West
  9.4% productivity improvement in the first year of gainsharing

- **Fabric conversion manufacturing**
  90 employees, West
  6.6% productivity improvement in the first year of gainsharing

- **Plastic injection molding and assembly**
  150 employees, northern Midwest
  Achieved a 15.4% productivity improvement two years after implementing gainsharing

PUCKETT STUDY

Eldridge Puckett[1] conducted a study in 1958 of productivity increases achieved in the two-year period after implementing gain-sharing at ten companies. The number of employees in the plants ranged from 30 in the smallest plant to 1,200 in the largest.

Productivity improvements in the first year ranged from 6.8% to 38.7%, with an average improvement of 22.5%. In the second year, productivity improvements ranged from 10.9% to 49.4%, with an average improvement of 23.7%. Over the two years, productivity improvements ranged from 10.3% to 39.2%, with an average productivity improvement of 23.1%.

Often companies are concerned that early productivity improvements may be achieved by harvesting low-hanging fruit and that further gains are difficult or not possible to achieve.

It's been my experience that gains continue to increase over time, as this study demonstrates.

US GENERAL ACCOUNTING OFFICE (GAO) EVALUATION OF GAINSHARING

The GAO's study[2] of gainsharing and other productivity-sharing programs reported that the use of gainsharing programs in private industry had resulted in significant productivity improvements.

---

[1] Eldridge S. Puckett, "Productivity Achievements—A Measure of Success," in *The Scanlon Plan: A Frontier in Labor-Management Cooperation*, ed. Frederick G. Lesieur, MIT Press, 1958.

[2] General Accounting Office, *Productivity Sharing Programs: Can They Contribute to Productivity Improvement?*, AFMD–81–22, March 3, 1981.

Many of the firms in the GAO review attributed significant work-force savings to their productivity-sharing plans: "Savings averaged 17.3% at the thirteen firms with annual sales of less than $100 million. At the other eleven firms, annual sales were $110 million or greater, and savings averaged 16.4%," the report said.

Of the twenty-four firms providing financial data, those with a productivity-sharing system for the longest period of time showed the best performance. Firms that had plans in operation for more than five years averaged almost 29% savings in workforce costs for the most recent five-year period, with individual firms' average savings ranging from 13.5% to 77.4%.

Those firms with plans in operation for less than five years averaged savings of 8.5 percent.

This data supports the contention that the financial benefits from productivity-sharing systems continue to grow over time and are an effective long-term strategy to improve organizational performance.

R.J. BULLOCK STUDY

An additional study of thirty-three gainsharing programs[3] by R.J. Bullock reported:

> Eighty percent of the companies reported measurable improvements in some hard measure of productivity, cost savings, or quality.
>
> Many of these gains were remarkable, ranging from 20% to 30%, with some gains even larger.

---

[3] R.J. Bullock, "Gainsharing—A Successful Track Record," World of Work Report, Volume 9 Number 8, August 1984, p 3.

About three-quarters of the companies studied reported
that some index of quality of work-life improved, such as a
decline in grievances, improvement in satisfaction or morale,
or an enhanced work climate.

Learn how to put the fundamentals in place to 1) motivate your employees, 2) focus everyone in your company on the high-leverage factors that drive business success, and 3) simplify the complexities of your business down to an understandable message where everyone in the company is on the same page and focused on high-leverage issues.

It's important to focus on what's required to jump-start positive, measurable gains and to sustain or increase them over time. You'll understand the processes and action steps other companies have used to achieve significant, lasting improvement and success.

But you must take action to start reaping the benefits.

OPPORTUNITY COST

There is a real risk in waiting to start gainsharing. As Bullock reported, "Dramatic improvements in productivity, cost, savings, and quality are reported in four out of five companies with gainsharing plans."

That's an 80% success rate, so there's reason to believe that your company could achieve significant gains, too. A delay in taking action would, thus, mean lost gains and opportunities. If your competitors take action, they could achieve a competitive advantage over you that may be hard to overcome.

Let's get into the basics of gainsharing, its essential parts, and how it transforms companies so that you can start reaping its benefits.

Target-Reward Mismatch

"If you measure the wrong thing, and then you reward the wrong thing, don't be surprised if you get the wrong thing."

Lee Copeland,
architect and urban designer

COMPANIES ARE EVALUATED on measures like sales growth, on-time delivery, cost reductions, and profits. They want to drive the measures and the numbers on which they're evaluated and that they use to keep score, so to speak.

But here's the problem. Companies want better performance. But their employees' pay isn't tied to or determined by performance.

Most employees get paid for their time. So there's a sizable mismatch between what companies want from employees and the way their employees are rewarded. Companies want one set of outcomes (performance, etc.). But they reward employees for and measure something different (their time).

The struggle to motivate their employees stems from a mismatch that could be eliminated.

WHAT DO EMPLOYEES WANT?

Employees' pay is often calculated directly from their time, their work hours. So they focus on the time they've put in because this determines how much their paycheck will be. Even salaried employees are expected to put in their time.

> **COMPANIES WANT BETTER PERFORMANCE. BUT THEIR EMPLOYEES' PAY ISN'T TIED TO OR DETERMINED BY PERFORMANCE.**

And because employees get paid for their time, they have no motivation, self-interest, or accountability to drive the measures and results management is focused on.

This creates fertile ground for people to stop focusing on getting results and driving the results the company needs.

WHY ARE YOUR PEOPLE ALWAYS BEHIND?

Ironically, because employees get paid for time, it's in their self-interest to be slightly behind.

They know that if they finish early, they might be sent home. If they get caught up, management begins wondering if they can get by with fewer hours or fewer people.

If workers are behind, it looks like they're working harder, carrying a greater burden. If they get caught up, they're not needed as much. The farther behind they are, the bigger the raise they can push for. If they leave for another employer, management would really be in a fix. They're considered indispensable. So why would they ever want to get caught up?

It gets worse.

If workers are eligible for overtime, they get a 50% bonus (overtime pay) to put in additional time to address urgent issues. The more problems, the more money they make. Companies want performance, but they end up paying workers more if they don't perform. Seems counterintuitive, doesn't it?

I'm not trying to imply that employees are doing anything intentionally improper here. They're just following the system and the rules the company has put in place.

But this situation sets up a mismatch between what a company wants and what it's rewarding.

Management wants workers to perform as though they have skin in the game, but it doesn't give them skin in the game. Companies want workers to think and act like high-performance athletes. But workers' pay is disconnected from their performance and company performance measures.

No wonder driving performance is such a struggle.

This is not entirely the companies' fault. In the United States, the Fair Labor Standards Act requires that certain employees be paid overtime. So companies have no choice but to pay overtime where this law applies.

The problem is this creates a conflict, a mismatch between what a company wants and how employees are rewarded.

Gainsharing brings the employees and the company closer together by focusing everyone on the same goals. Achieving gainsharing goals drives both the company's financial measures and the employees' bonuses. So both the company and the employees are rewarded by achieving or surpassing these goals.

Sage Oil Vac President Aaron Sage puts it this way:

> It doesn't work to talk to employees in terms of overhead, overhead percentages, in-depth financial concepts that the business owner, accountant, and the banker wants to see.

Gainsharing gives them a goal, and they can see weekly [whether] they're above or below the goal. That puts it in terms of "we're doing well or we're not doing well." And so... inherently, everybody wants to do well, right? No one wants to do badly. They want the company to do well, and they want to do well. They want to know that they're doing well. And if you break it down weekly in terms of a number, and they see that they're above or below the number, then they can have faith that the rest of everything they don't understand as much is going well.

So I think that's where you get past the mismatch. You know they see their monthly results; they got a gainshare, or they didn't get a gainshare. If they didn't get a gainshare, you know, two things are bad. One, they didn't get an extra bonus. And two, they know that we need to pick it up in some area to get that bonus. And so that's what motivates them.

They get more involved in the week-to-week gainsharing goals because they want to hit it again. And then that's why they keep talking about it with their coworkers.

HOW TO FIX THIS MISMATCH

Here's how to put the must-have elements in place to fix this mismatch.

We will, of course, go into greater detail later, but, for now, this is **an overview of how we fix this mismatch**:

- First, we get the company and employees focused on the most important financial (P&L) line items that drive the profits of the company. This gives everyone—company and employees—common goals and successes.
- We tie rewards (bonuses) to beating the common goals. This way, everyone wins together.

- We clearly define what "good" looks like. That is, we clearly define whether we are going to have good performance in a day, week, month, or year, and what that looks like specifically. This gives everyone a big-picture goal.
- We give real-time feedback regarding how performance affects goals.
- We provide specific action plans that give daily to-do lists for employees that tie back to the big goal. This tells them what they need to complete today to do their part in achieving the overall goals.
- We spell out the needs for fixes and system improvements.

These elements work together to get everyone pulling in the same direction, unite their self-interest, and reward their common successes.

SUMMARY

In many companies, employee self-interest is in direct conflict with company self-interest. They have different, conflicting goals.

Companies struggle to motivate their employees because employee self-interest is tied to the hours employees put in. Motivation is not tied to achieving company goals.

This can be fixed.

NEXT UP: THE BEST STEPS TO DO SO.

2

Six Steps

"Success is neither magical nor mysterious.
Success is the natural consequence of
consistently applying basic fundamentals."

Jim Rohn,
author and entrepreneur

DURING A TOUR of a manufacturing plant a couple years ago, it occurred to me as the tour progressed that my mind was going down a checklist evaluating whether certain features or items were in place.

I've learned through implementing many gainsharing systems, there are certain essential features that need to be in place for gainsharing to be successful. Each of the must-have parts of the gainsharing process adds to and gains from the momentum of the other parts.

As the tour progressed, I was evaluating, "Are there any essential pieces missing?"

Success with gainsharing is straightforward. In a cause-and-effect world, if you do what others have done, you'll achieve the same results they've achieved.

We know from successful gainsharing systems, the necessary pieces that need to be in place, or steps that need to be followed to be successful. If you put the necessary pieces in place, you'll be on track to achieve the same success other companies have achieved.

These six pieces give you the code, or recipe, to create motivated employees, pulling in the same direction and driving performance.

These essentials of the gainsharing process are organized into six pieces, which form the foundation of our gainsharing model. The result is a comprehensive system to drive business fundamentals and motivation, and leverage proven principles of human behavior.

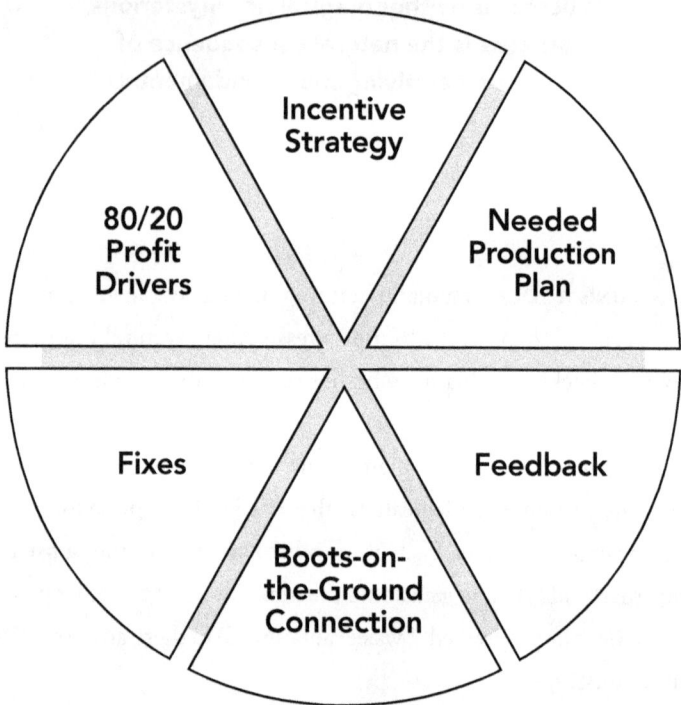

FIGURE 1: *The six essential steps of the gainsharing model.*

THE SIX PIECES, BRIEFLY

80/20 profit drivers

- In every company's financials, there are high-leverage line items that also drive other line items.
- By driving these high-leverage items, we drive profits.
- The complexity of company financials becomes simplicity.

Incentive strategy

- Once we've clarified the company profit drivers, we tie bonuses to driving these high-leverage items.
- This gets everybody pulling in the same direction.
- And it creates a win-win for both company and employees.

Needed Production Plan

- The Needed Production Plan specifies what needs to happen at a zoomed out 30,000-foot level for the company to have a terrific week, month, and so on. This plan outlines what it will take to be on the hunt for a gainsharing bonus.
- It's a big-picture plan that also clarifies the plan components needed to achieve success, and, crucially, it gets everybody on the same page.

Feedback

- The feedback process reveals how things are coming together compared to the plan.
- It also sets up the information and structure for employees to be accountable.
- This helps pull everyone together since they're using the same feedback and information in order to make adjustments to hit goals they're targeting together.

Boots-on-the-Ground Connection

- Employees need to know what they have to do today to carry their weight and earn their bonus.
- They need specifics.
- And they need feedback about how well they're doing as they go through their day, week, or month so they can make adjustments in real time.
- This connects everyone (both company and employees) to the performance needed to hit their common goals.

Fixes

- The fixes address the gaps between targets and results so that performance is better in the future.
- The gains largely come from implementing the fixes.
- The fixes are examples of employees and management moving together with a united focus in order to make money and address the challenges of business.

NEXT UP: WE'LL FOCUS ON THE REWARDS FOR FOCUSING ON THE FACTORS WE SEE AS THE 80/20 DRIVERS.

3

80/20 Profit Drivers

**"If you don't know where you are going,
you might wind up someplace else."**

Yogi Berra

THE MOST IMPORTANT issue in designing an effective gainsharing system is to make sure bonuses track with profits.

That is, when bonuses are paid, the company is achieving or beating an acceptable profit. This leads to one of my core principles: **The more bonus is paid, the stronger the profits should be.**

This is essential because, when it's in place, everything we do to drive gainsharing simultaneously drives company performance.

If you don't have this in place, then gainsharing becomes a side effort, something that's nice to achieve but not a must.

When this is in place, gainsharing performance indicates whether we're on track to beat the company's profit goal. It's like the instruments in an airplane indicating that your airplane is losing altitude. This has its own urgency.

A sense of urgency is essential to keeping the spark alive over time. It's essential that people see there's no slip in the gears, that the things we do to drive gainsharing also drive the other essential outcomes.

An idea is a good idea if it's a shortcut to what needs be done anyway. We want everything we do through gainsharing to drive results we'd have to achieve without gainsharing. It's essential people see a direct through line between what they're doing on a day-to-day basis to drivng gainsharing results and overall company objectives and profits.

Let's look at a graphic illustration of profits and bonuses tracking together.

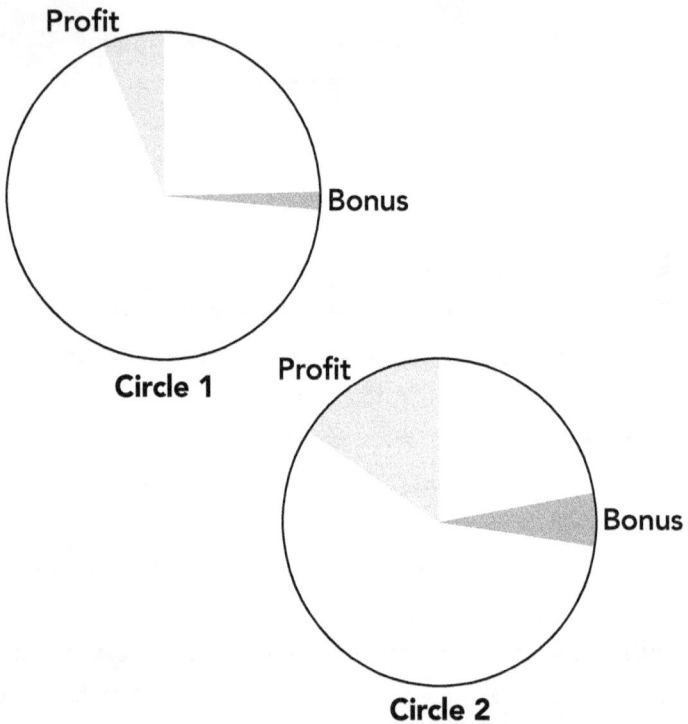

FIGURE 2: *Profits and bonuses track together.*

In Figure 2, as we compare the change from Circle 1 to Circle 2, we see both the company's profit and the employees' bonuses increase at similar rates. That is, the pieces of the pie vary together. Both pieces of the pie should be getting bigger or both getting smaller.

But most people think that if their pay is going to increase (bonus piece gets bigger), then the company's profit is getting smaller, as though money is shifting from one piece of the pie to the other. That is, one piece gets smaller as the other gets bigger.

But with the gainsharing formula, we see equanimity: Both are increasing or decreasing at the same time.

When we set up the formula this way, everything we do to drive the gainsharing results on a day-by-day basis also drives business results.

This is the core issue for a formula. That is, there needs to be a relationship between changes in the central measures in the formula and changes in the company's bottom line.

PARETO PRINCIPLE

Building a formula this way follows the Pareto Principle. Vilfredo Pareto[4] was an Italian economist who lived in the late 1800s. He noticed that most of the wealth in his country was in the hands of a few people. That is, 80% of the money was in the hands of 20% of the people.

This Pareto Principle, also known as the 80/20 Rule, applies to many situations. For example, it's quite common for 80% of a company's sales revenue to come from 20% of its customers. And the remaining 20% of the company's revenue comes from 80% of its customers.

But it also applies to other areas of our lives:

- Of the frustrating encounters you have with other people in your life, 80% probably occur with 20% of the people you know.
- Of the weight you gain, probably 80% comes from 20% of the food you eat.

---

[4]   Geoffrey Duncan Mitchell. *A Hundred Years of Sociology*. Transaction Publishers, 1968. p. 115.

I'm having a bit of fun here, but you get the idea. This concept has broad applicability. But it's very important in developing an effective, easy-to-live-with gainsharing formula.

HOW THIS APPLIES TO GAINSHARING

In every company's financials, there are a few line items that drive many other items. So if you can control or influence these driver elements, you're influencing a long list of other items simultaneously through these lever items.

For example, many financial controllers know their company is going to have a good profit month, if they have:

- A certain level of production or sales volume, and
- Material costs are at this percentage of sales or less, and
- Labor costs are this amount or less.

Since these factors drive so many other factors, if you know where the company stands in a given month on these driver factors, you can predict the final profit levels, or at least whether the company will be having a good profit month or not.

For example, high levels of direct labor or overtime can be significant costs on their own. But when more hours are worked, whether they are direct labor hours or overtime hours, people are spending money in many ways. Hopefully, they're not just standing still but in motion and spending money. They're using utilities. They're using materials. So when these labor costs increase, many other costs increase as well. The combined effect can be massive.

There are a few vital categories that have significant influence and drive overall results. The result of this is: A majority of a company's profits are often caused by a minority of the cost factors or line items in the company's financials.

By finding these factors and putting them at the center of your gainsharing formula, you'll transform the complexity of your P&L to simplicity. Driving these high-leverage factors drives the bottom line.

Earl Chupp, President of Woodenware says this about using gainsharing's 80/20 principle:

> You're only focused on the things that matter. All this busy stuff that we thought was important really wasn't that important. We were just doing things to stay busy. But once we understood these levers, if you pull these levers in the company, that's where you're going to get your meat and your potatoes from. And so you focus on those, and you get all your employees focused on those. . . . . [After] a while, you're printing money. I mean, it just doesn't take long.

PREDICTS FINANCIAL STATEMENTS

One of the benefits of having the formula set up so gainsharing results and bonuses track with profits is that your weekly gainsharing results predict financial performance. That is, gainsharing results on a week-by-week basis predict profits for the month.

This adds to the importance the feedback gainsharing provides. It's like when the instruments in an airplane show you're losing altitude, and you can see the ground is getting closer. It has its own urgency.

My clients have told me this is very useful because they don't get their financial statements in a given month until a week or two after the month ends. This allows them to know if their plane is losing altitude before it's too late to pull up. The gainsharing information gives feedback week by week throughout the month so they're able to make corrections during the flight, so to speak.

Steve Hicks, President of Dongan Electric says:

> [Gainsharing] really has, over time, come to be the front and center metric. And then, of course, financial statements follow on after that, which sort of verify what we're seeing. So I think it is the central metric of value to this company, even without knowing financials.

BONUSES MUST BE SELF-FUNDING

By setting up the gainsharing formula so it's focused on the factors that drive the bottom line, we're also setting things up for bonuses to be naturally self-funded.

That is, we don't pay a bonus until performance is beyond a threshold point. Both the bonuses and bottom line are being driven by performance on the central gainsharing measures.

Since we don't pay bonuses until performance is beyond the targeted levels, the problem isn't paying bonuses when we're beating the targets. It's when we're not paying bonuses. Because when we're not paying bonuses, that means the performance isn't up to levels that deliver or exceed the targeted profits.

Chupp says, in his experience, there has been what amounts to about a 30-60 split between what the employees get versus what the company gets when gainsharing is paid.

This is how Chupp breaks it down:

> So for every dollar of gainshare that you're making, 30% of it goes to employees and 60% goes to the company. That's about what I've noticed. Yeah, it's a 30-60 trade-

off. So when they're hitting the gainshare, when they're ringing gainshare, you know, you're making money if your numbers are right. Why wouldn't you want them to make gainshare money? Life is not good when you're not paying out gainshare.

GET EVERYONE WORKING TOGETHER

When bonuses and profits track together, the company and people are in it together, as opposed to working at opposite objectives or in a tug-of-war.

Employees typically think the company wants to minimize bonuses paid. When we implement a gainsharing system, there's often an unstated fear the company is going to make the goals more difficult as employees start earning sizable bonuses.

What's more, there's often a fear that goals will ratchet up and be increasingly difficult. Employees assume when they achieve bonuses, things will get increasingly difficult to the point where the bonuses are no longer achievable. They think this is standard operating procedure and that this is what the company wants to do.

In other words, employees fear that the company doesn't really want to pay bonuses, and once they are paying bonuses, they'll make the goals more difficult to avoid continuing to pay bonuses.

But when your gainsharing or pay-for-performance system is set up properly, this is not true.

It's important employees understand this is not true. We need to proactively eliminate this misperception up front and get this misunderstanding straightened out. When gainsharing is designed correctly, everyone is together in winning or not winning.

When we set things up so both profits and bonuses track with one another, the company wants to be paying the bonuses every period, or as often as possible. Why? Because this means they're exceeding not only targeted performance but profit levels, too.

In effect, the company and employees both get a bonus.

WHAT DO WE INCLUDE IN THE FORMULA?

When we design a formula, one of the first questions that comes up is, "So what do we include in the formula?" My answer is that we can't include everything because we can't focus on everything. It's a contradiction. So we must leave something out.

The problem here is that a dollar saved in any P&L line item is a good thing. So how do we decide not to include a given cost category in the formula?

How do we sort through what will be included and what will not be included in the formula?

WHICH FORMULA FORMAT TO USE?

The second issue is: What formula arrangement should be used? The selected P&L line items can be put together in different formula formats. If I had three formulas, and one of them was better, how would I know? How would I recognize the best formula format if I were looking at it?

We can say, for example, we're going to have total sales, material costs, labor costs, and utilities in the formula. But there are many different ways those can be combined into a formula.

So if I had three formulas and one of them was better, how would I know? What am I looking for? And how would I recognize the best formula?

MICHELANGELO'S *DAVID*

Whenever I think of this issue, it reminds me of a story about Michelangelo carving the *David*, pictured below.

Legend has it that someone asked him, "How did you carve the statue?" He replied, "Well I got a big piece of marble, and then I took off everything that was not the statue. And there it was."

This basic thought process can be used to sort through what should be included in the gainsharing formula.

To do so, you start with the complete P&L of the company and remove items that don't have a relationship with profits; "a direct relationship" means that when the item that's considered changes, the profits change, too. So you whittle away the factors that don't have this lever relationship and are left with factors that drive the bottom line.

Doing so uncovers the 80/20 factors in a company's financials that are driving the bottom line.

It's like working a lever where changes in a given factor have a consistent, predictable relationship to changes in the company's bottom line. So you're looking for the factors that have a demonstrated, consistent relationship with profits, where changes in that factor correspond to changes in the company's bottom line.

These are the factors that you want to be the centerpiece of the gainsharing formula. Then, when you focus on these factors, you're driving the company's bottom line with everything that you do and every focus that you exert on the gainsharing operations.

OFFSET CROSS-PURPOSES

There are so many things in companies that get people pulling in different directions. It's important to have structures to offset this tendency for employees to have conflicting agendas and to be working at cross-purposes.

There are many ways to put a gainsharing formula together. But when done effectively, it gets everybody in the company pulling in the same direction and rewards their shared success.

This alignment goes a long way toward eliminating the mismatch between what employees want and what the company wants. This gets everyone focused on the same goals and sharing the rewards when the goals are achieved. Everyone is pulling in the same direction and success is a true win-win situation.

SUMMARY

We want to focus the gainsharing formula and measures on the financial elements that drive company financial results. That way, everything a company does with gainsharing to drive performance and pay bonuses also drives company self-interest and the bottom line.

Also, when the formula is designed this way, gainsharing is driving the performance a company needs, whether it has gainsharing or not.

This helps keep the spark alive over time and helps a company keep its eye on the ball. And because gainsharing focuses on driving the high-leverage issues and performance needed, even if the company doesn't have a gainsharing system, gainsharing never loses its validity.

NEXT UP: WE'LL EXAMINE THE TYPES OF FORMULAS IN DETAIL.

4

Formula Types

"Any professional sports coach will tell you: Measurement automatically improves performance, and measurement monitored by someone else further improves performance."

Dan Kennedy,
marketing expert

OF COURSE, ONE of the main objectives of a gainsharing system is to drive gains. These gains are measured and tracked by the gainsharing formula.

Because the formula defines the improvements, which will lead to bonuses, the measures in the formula are a key focus of employee attention. As the old saying goes, "What gets measured gets done." So the design of the formula is very important.

Let's review some of the common options.

GAINSHARING IS NOT PROFIT SHARING

Profit sharing is a type of pay-for-performance system. People often use the terms profit sharing and gainsharing interchangeably. The confusion is understandable. But, to be clear, they are not the same.

For example:

- Both profit sharing and gainsharing pay bonuses.
- Profits are gains.
- Both have the term "sharing" in their names.

So gainsharing and profit sharing may seem like they're largely the same. But profit sharing and gainsharing are very different in their ability to motivate, guide, and drive performance.

Companies often want to give people an incentive to work harder and smarter.

They also want to reward people when performance is there, but they avoid getting locked into high levels of guaranteed pay.

Companies want to be sure the company is beating profit goals before they pay a bonus. That is, they don't want to be in a situation where bonuses are expected when the company isn't actually doing better. So they wait until the final profits have been calculated and then share a certain portion.

Because they want a simple system where bonuses track with profits, they often choose a profit-sharing system.

They believe using profit sharing this way, gives them an effective incentive system. The problem is profit sharing isn't an incentive system and probably won't incentivize their people at all.

Why not? Profit sharing typically involves distributing a portion of the profits to employees as a bonus, often at the end of the year. People don't get much information throughout the year, except possibly some updates about the profit levels year-to-date and the prospects for a payout.

Profit sharing shares the profits after the fact, but it does little to guide performance.

It doesn't tell people what to do to drive the gains. It just shares the gains once they are achieved.

Profit sharing doesn't work well as an incentive because typically:

- People don't know what they did to create the profits, and
- They don't know what they need to do to carry their weight to earn a bonus.

There usually aren't profit-sharing communication routines or meetings throughout the year to talk about problems, how to attack them, and how to drive gains.

Since employees don't see how their efforts had an impact on profits, it's unlikely bonus payouts influence future behavior.

Because there's a great disconnect between what people do and profit-sharing bonuses, profit sharing provides little incentive or no incentive at all. There's a disconnect because people don't see the connection between what they do and the rewards they get.

THE PROBLEM IS PROFIT SHARING ISN'T AN INCENTIVE SYSTEM AND PROBABLY WON'T INCENTIVIZE THEIR PEOPLE. . . AT ALL.

This can lead to great disappointment since the company may be paying significant bonuses but not getting the impact they're seeking.

Also, profit sharing shares the profits after they've occurred.

The focus is on the past—where you've been. It's like driving a car when you can only see out the rear window.

Imagine you had one of those sunshades on your windshield that people unfold to block the sun when their car is parked. Then imagine you had to drive forward, but you could only see out the back window to guide your driving. In contrast, a true incentive system aims to influence future behavior. You are, thus, driving the car looking out the front windshield.

Motivation matters, and an effective incentive or gainsharing system motivates. They share the following features:

- People know what the overall goal or needed production is.
- They know what they need to do to achieve their part of the goal.
- They believe their efforts will yield the results they want.
- They get monthly, weekly, daily, or perhaps hourly real-time feedback as they work towards their goal.
- And they identify certain results (bonuses, visibility, friendly rivalries, and more) that are important to them, and they tie these to regarding themselves as successful. In this way, the results become personal.

Although money is an important reward, it's not the only reward, or even the most important in many instances.

People want to see they're making an important contribution, that they're seen as carrying their weight and are part of something bigger than themselves.

The real key to an effective gainsharing or incentive system is transforming work into a game where employees are driving results because it's important to them personally.

When this happens, people drive the performance whether anyone is watching them or not because they want to do it for themselves.

When we can make these deeper connections, bonuses are the response to the question, "I see the company is doing better, but what do I get out of this?" Bonuses close that circle, and we've successfully motivated people on many levels.

It's not as though profit sharing is bad or undesirable. Often companies have both a gainsharing and profit-sharing system. There's no inherent conflict between the two.

Profit sharing does provide a financial benefit. It can be very effective for many purposes. For instance, profit sharing can be an effective way to fund retirement vehicles. It's just not an effective tool to motivate or incentivize employees.

LABOR-TO-SALES FORMAT

Labor to sales is one of the simplest formula formats. It focuses on total pay and benefit costs (people costs) in ratio to sales.

This formula can work well in service companies, where people costs are significant and can be 50% to 65% of total revenue.

It also can work well in companies with very low material costs, such as a dry cleaner.

The heart of the formula calculation is the ratio of total pay and benefits to total sales, expressed as a percentage (Figure 3).

$$\frac{\text{People Costs (Payroll \& Fringes)}}{\text{Total Sales}} = x\%$$

FIGURE 3: *People costs-to-sales ratio.*

The actual percentage of total people costs to sales in a given period is compared to a targeted percentage.

In row 3 of Figure 4 (page 40), we can see the targeted people costs have been calculated at 30% of total sales.

In row 10, we see total people costs subtracted from targeted people costs resulting in the bonus pool of 6,000.

1.	**Total Sales**	350,000
2.	**Threshold**	30%
3.	**Targeted People Costs**	105,000
4.	**Regular Pay**	76,000
5.	**Overtime Pay**	2,000
6.	**Vacation Pay**	2,000
7.	**Holiday Pay**	3,000
8.	**Health Insurance**	16,000
9.	**Total People Costs**	99,000
10.	**105,000 – 99,000**	6,000

FIGURE 4: *Labor-to-sales formula*

The bonus percentage calculation is shown in Figure 5. The bonus pool (line 1) is divided by the total of regular pay plus overtime pay (line 2). Each eligible employee would receive 7.7% of their pay as bonus.

$$\frac{\text{1.} \quad 6,000}{\text{2.} \quad 78,000} = 7.7\%$$

FIGURE 5: *Bonus percentage*

VALUE PRODUCED

The value-produced formula focuses on the value of production as a ratio of total people costs.

Stated briefly, production value can be measured as (1) total sales plus or minus changes in finished goods inventory, or (2) total sales plus or minus changes in finished goods inventory *and* changes in work-process inventory.

In Figure 6, line 3 is the combination of sales, plus an increase in inventory, which may be finished goods inventory or finished goods inventory plus work-in-process inventory.

Lines 4 and 5 are adjustments subtracted from line three. Line 4 could be the value of customer returns. Line 5 might be plating, painting, machining, or other outside services that added value to production but were not done by the gainsharing-eligible group. Sometimes, not all employees are eligible to receive gainsharing bonuses. For example, the office people, support people (maintenance, etc.). The company decides during the gainsharing design process which employees will be eligible for bonuses.

The targeted people costs (line 8) are calculated by multiplying line 6 by the threshold percentage (line 7).

The bonus pool is shown in line 15, which subtracts total people costs from targeted people costs.

1.	Total Sales	330,000
2.	Inventory Changes +(-)	50,000
3.		380,000
	LESS:	
4.	Returns	5,000
5.	Outside Services	2,000
		373,000
7.	Threshold	30%
8.	Targeted People Costs	111,900
9.	Regular Pay	76,000
10.	Overtime Pay	2,000
11.	Vacation Pay	2,000
12.	Holiday Pay	3,000
13.	Health Insurance	16,000
14.	Total People Costs	99,000
15.	105,000 – 99,000	6,000

FIGURE 6: *Value-produced formula*

VALUE ADDED

The value-added formula format differs from the labor-to-sales and value-produced formulas in that it includes material costs in the calculation.

Material costs are subtracted from value produced (or sales), which results in value added.

Because material costs are subtracted from value produced (or sales) and the remainder is value added, changes in material costs result in changes in value added. For example, material cost savings can result in an improved value-added number because a lower material cost was subtracted from value produced, or sales.

Including material cost changes in the formula calculation can make a big difference in formula effectiveness. This is not always the case though. Any addition to the formula adds complexity, so there's always a benefit-to-increased-complexity trade-off.

Value added is very effective at handling what are called "mix issues." These are situations where, for example, you make a lot of money on one product, but not on another. Or where material costs are very different in one product category versus another. Value -added formulas can be very effective at handling these mix issues.

It's like the suspension on your car and how it handles the variations in the road as you drive. The suspension allows your tires to move up and down quite a bit. But as you drive along, your perception is that the road is smooth. The suspension does a good job of addressing these variations in the road. A value-added formula often works the same way to properly address variations in product mix, material costs, and more.

In Figure 7, line 6 shows material costs included with the items that are subtracted from line 3.

Because material is being subtracted, increases in material costs with no changes in line 3 will result in a reduction in line 7.

Line 7 is multiplied by the threshold (line 8) to give the targeted people costs. So increases in the "material costs" line flow through to a reduction in line 9.

The point here is that higher scrap rates, lower material yield, etc., lead directly to reductions in the bonus pool (line 16). Conversely, savings and improvements in material-related issues lead to increases in the bonus pool.

So people are directly tied to doing the best they can on material performance, just as they would be if this were their company.

1.	Total Sales	330,000
2.	Inventory Changes +(-)	50,000
3.		380,000
	LESS:	
4.	Returns	5,000
5.	Outside Services	2,000
6.	Material	100,073
7.		272,927
8.	Threshold	41%
9.	Targeted People Costs	111,900
10.	Regular Pay	76,000
11.	Overtime Pay	2,000
12.	Vacation Pay	2,000
13.	Holiday Pay	3,000
14.	Health Insurance	16,000
15.	Total People Costs	99,000
16.	111,900 – 99,000	6,000

FIGURE 7: *Value-added formula*

SPLIT RATIO

Sometimes the people costs as a percent of value added, value produced, or sales are so different from one product group to another that it makes sense to have more than one threshold or target people cost.

This explains why total people costs of one product group are significantly different from those of another product group.

Briefly, this means, "More of this is not the same as more of that."

This formula format sets up several streams to properly adjust and calculate the appropriate targets, based on the products being produced.

Line 3 shows the production as a combination of sales plus or minus changes in finished goods inventory for product groups A, B, and total production.

Line 5 shows the material costs for product groups A and B. The material costs for these two groups are significantly different. The material cost percentages for the individual product groups, as a percent of production, are shown in line 4.

Line 6 is a placeholder for the cost of quality charges. This might include costs like charge-backs from customers and the like for quality problems.

Line 7 is a placeholder for premium freight to be subtracted.

Line 8 is a spot for unusual or one-time charges to be entered into the calculation. This is a place where items can be spotlighted for attention and discussion. Without this placeholder line, there wouldn't be a place to spotlight these special, one-time charges for discussion and problem-solving.

Line 9 shows the calculation of value added as the total of lines 5 through 8, subtracted from line 3.

Value added, for each of the two product groups, is multiplied by the individual thresholds to show the target people costs in line 11.

Line 19 shows the total people costs subtracted from the total target people costs (Line 11) to calculate the bonus pool.

		Product Group A	Product Group B	Total
1.	Sales	219,534	850,000	1,069,534
2.	FG Inv Chg	(42,349)	87,129	44,780
3.	Production	177,185	937,129	1,114,314
4.	Mat % Production	72%	44%	
	LESS:			
5.	Material	127,573	417,022	544,595
6.	Cost of Quality Changes	0	0	0
7.	Premium Freight	0	763	763
8.	Other Adj	0	0	0
9.	Value Added	49,612	519,344	568,956
10.	Threshold	53.40%	59.15%	
11.	Target People Costs	26,493	307,192	333,685
12.	Regular Pay			231,517
13.	Overtime			20,132
14.	Temps			2,516
15.	Vacation			11,576
16.	Holiday			10,821
17.	Health Ins			38,955
18.	Total People Costs			315,517
19.	Gainsharing Earned (Lost)			18,168

FIGURE 8: *Split-ratio formula*

ALLOWED LABOR

Allowed labor formulas are basically a comparison of actual labor costs to a standard, or allowed labor cost (Figure 9).

Allowed Labor Cost

Less

Actual Labor Costs

FIGURE 9: *Allowed labor formulas represent a comparison of allowed vs. actual labor costs.*

This comparison can be very useful and informative, but it is subject to all the frustrations common with piecework systems.

For example, the allowed labor or standard labor must be calculated and kept in proper adjustment. It's easy for these standards to fall out of adjustment. And since employees' pay is tied to performance in comparison to the standards, management may be hesitant to make adjustments to the standards.

In recent times, many manufacturing companies have changed from a situation where they make the same thing over and over to what is called a job-shop environment. An allowed labor formula is best suited to situations where you're making the same thing over and over.

We see an example calculation in Figure 10.

Line 1 shows that the standard hours needed to produce 4,000 units of product equals 40,000 hours.

But the total actual hours, which would include indirect hours, such as maintenance, shipping, and setup, equals 60,000 hours.

Line 3 shows the BPF, or the base productivity factor, which represents the ratio between the total actual hours and the standard hours.

The BPF is used as a multiplier to calculate the total allowed hours to produce a given number of units from the standard hours.

So if the hours to produce 4,000 units was 38,500 hours, then, when we multiply by the BPF, the total actual hours would be 57,750 (Line 4).

The bonus hours would be calculated by subtracting 57,750 from 60,000 (Line 5).

Line 6 shows the calculation of the bonus percentage as the ratio between the bonus hours and the total actual hours.

The bonus calculation for an individual worker would be calculated as their hours worked (Line 7), multiplied by the bonus percentage (Line 6) to get their bonus hours (Line 9). These bonus hours (Line 9) would then be multiplied by the worker's pay rate (Line 8) to get their individual bonus (Line 10).

1.	**Standard hours to produce 4,000 units**	**40,000**
2.	**Total actual hours to produce 4,000 units** (**Actual hours are higher because they include shipping, maintenance, setup hours, etc.**)	**60,000**
3.	**BPF = 60,000/40,000**	**1.5**
4.	**If actual hours = 38,500 x 1.5 (BPF)**	**57,750**
5.	**Then, bonus hours = 60,000 - 57,750**	**2,250 hours**
6.	**Bonus = 2,250/57,750 = 3.896%**	
	Bonus calculation for an individual worker	
7.	**Hours worked**	**160**
8.	**Pay rate**	**$15.00 per hour**
9.	**Bonus hours (3.896% of 160 hours)**	**6.23 hours**
10.	**Bonus: 6.23 hours x $15.00**	**$93.45**

FIGURE 10: *Allowed-payroll formula*

FAMILY OF MEASURES

Family-of-measures formulas got their start as an offshoot from efforts to improve productivity in white-collar settings. This type of formula uses a format that's often used for management compensation.

In a management-by-objectives (MBO) format, a manager may be hired to achieve certain outcomes. This manager may have a base pay, or salary, but the majority of their pay may be tied to achieving certain defined objectives.

So this person has a salary, but they have really been hired to achieve certain measured outcomes. In addition to their base pay, they receive bonuses tied to achieving these outcomes.

Since management and executive compensation is frequently structured this way, this is a format they're immediately familiar and comfortable with.

Family-of-measures formulas follow a similar format, in that they specify the most important items to be tracked and measured, and they tie rewards to their achievement (see Figure 11).

**Captures the Elements That
Make Up Performance in a Company**

**Builds Them Into a Formula Usually
Based on Antipated Savings**

FIGURE 11: *Broadly, how a family-of-measures formula works.*

In designing a family-of-measures system, we start with defining what we think productivity is in a given company. This might include productivity, quality, safety, and customer complaints (see Figure 11). We put together a way to measure each of these individual things and a way to show improvements in each of these individual measurements. We put together a way to combine these savings and to calculate a bonus if performance improves. This becomes the centerpiece of the formula.

This does require that we maintain each of the elements in the formula, which can lead to a situation where you have a formula that requires more maintenance and adjustments than other types of formulas.

Management can be hesitant about changing the goals or formula calculations when employee pay is tied to this calculation, just as companies are often hesitant to adjust the goals or the standards in a piecework system once the system is underway.

On the positive side, though, a family-of-measures formula gives feedback on the measures that are deemed useful and important.

Productivity	**Labor and benefits as a percent of sales**
Scrap	**Scrap cost as a percent of sales**
Schedule Attainment	**Value of scheduled production, less missed orders/scheduled production**
Quality	**Number of defects expressed as parts per million**
Customer Complaints	**Number of credits issued to customers**

FIGURE 12: *Example of family-of-measures items.*

NEXT UP: A GAINSHARING FORMULA OUTLINES HOW GAINS ARE CALCULATED AND TRACKED. ONCE IN PLACE, WE SET UP REWARDS AND BONUSES FOR EMPLOYEES.

5

Incentive Strategy

"You basically get what you reward."

Stephen R. Covey,
American educator and author

ONCE EMPLOYEES HAVE made progress towards their gainsharing goals and company performance improves, it's inevitable they'll ask themselves whether they are better off. They wonder what they're getting out of this.

That's where gainsharing bonuses come in. Bonuses answer the employee question, "What do I get out of this?"

Many companies say they want to improve productivity and reward employees for extra effort and results. But when companies put a bonus system in place, it shows they're putting their money where their mouth is and are serious about wanting to improve performance and share the gains and improvements with employees.

WHAT MOTIVATES PEOPLE?

Motivation can seem complex. But stated simply: People do what they do to get what they want.

We want employees to put in extra effort, something beyond the minimum. But do we give them something extra for the extra effort they put in? Why would employees give extra effort for the same pay they'll get anyway?

Psychologists have demonstrated that if a person takes an action and then receives a reward tied to taking the action, they're more likely to take that action again in the future.

WHAT GETS REWARDED GETS REPEATED.

This is called positive reinforcement because the reward reinforces the connection between action and getting something that's wanted.

So bonuses not only answer the question "What's in it for me?" but also make it more likely that employees will enthusiastically take action to get bonuses again in the future.

Chupp of Woodenware notes, "When they get the gainshare payout in their pocket, when they feel that and get that, you're off to the races[. At that point], they just want more."

PLAY HARD, WORK HARD

As we've said, the bonus can answer the initial "What's in it for me?" question. But it also takes more to drive sustained high-level performance.

There's an old saying: "If you love what you do, you'll never have to work a day in your life."

When an employee's work is like a game to them, they drive results because it's important to them personally. We can set up that employee's work so that it pulls them in, captures their full attention, and keeps them engaged as though they're playing a game.

The people in Las Vegas certainly know how to build an environment to pull people in and keep them focused. Casinos are deliber-

ately designed with no clocks, no windows, and other factors that
have been scientifically proven to keep people engaged.

THREE FACTORS FOR REWARDS-DRIVEN WORK

Work can be designed to pull employees in and keep them focused.
There are three important factors in structuring work so they drive
results as though it's a game, much like playing a slot machine:

- **Take action.**
  First, the employee has to take action. Like the person
  pulling the lever on the slot machine, taking action pulls the
  employee into the process.

- **Get feedback.**
  Second, the employee has to get feedback, just as the sounds,
  lights, and motion from the slot machine do. These first two
  steps in taking action and getting feedback are more than
  80% of what it takes to make an activity mimic a game.

- **There should be a reward, something workers want.**
  Finally, being successful in carrying out their actions needs
  to be tied to something they want. Remember the underlying
  principle: Workers do what they do to get what they want.
  There needs to be a reward, something employees want to
  drive their actions.

We use these three principles in building a gainsharing system.
First, we're going to put together a plan that will have everyone on
track to earn a substantial bonus at the end of the gainsharing period,
which is typically one month.

Next, we're going to break down this overall plan to what has to happen where so that this overall performance can be achieved.

Then we're going to give everyone feedback throughout the weeks, and even throughout the day, looking at how they're doing, on their part, to achieve the overall goal. So we have people taking action and getting direct feedback on their actions.

Having objectives, taking action, and getting feedback makes work very much like a game. We may run out of a certain kind of production material or a certain machine may break down, but we still need to hit the overall number, which means the game isn't over yet. So I'm watching you, and you're watching me as we're struggling to produce the best performance and the best results.

When workers beat their gainsharing goals, they, of course, receive their bonus. And that has tremendous value. But there are many other things people want from their work that come along with beating the gainsharing goals: achievement, working together with others, showing that they are doing their part in a group working towards a common goal, showing that they are performing better than they have in the past, and more.

SWEAT EQUITY IS NOT THE POINT

Once employees receive a couple significant gainsharing bonuses, it's common for them to realize the bonus was earned more by things coming together better than it was from more effort or sweat equity.

It's not as though greater effort isn't involved. They may have had to hustle more at certain points during the gainsharing period when they earned a bonus. But it becomes apparent that the bonus was really driven more by smart planning and performance than by more work.

When employees stay focused on reaching gainsharing goals in their departments or areas and then making adjustments to address problems, performance will improve and, before long, they'll hit target numbers.

They'll realize doing this didn't require that much extra effort. They just need to "plan the work and work the plan" and make sure they're not struggling with the same problems over and over. This way, it becomes much easier to consistently hit target numbers.

Once the targeted gainsharing is achieved, the bonus has a flywheel-like effect, meaning it provides the momentum to do it again. It closes the circle and answers the employee question, "What do I get out of this?" Then the cycle repeats.

Once this becomes apparent, people realize they should be getting themselves organized and earning bonuses regularly. Eventually, it's normal to get a bonus and unusual when they don't.

HOW MUCH MONEY ARE WE TALKING?

The performance of some companies will improve enough in their very first gainsharing period to pay a bonus. Even if a company doesn't pay a bonus in their first gainsharing period, it's quite common to get a bonus within the first three periods.

These bonuses can range from very small to 7% or so of a person's pay. Sometimes bonuses can reach 10% or more. I've had clients who have paid a bonus for a month that was equal to another week's pay, but this is not typical.

IN BOTH THE COMPANY AND EMPLOYEE'S INTEREST

It should be noted that when employees strive to make gainsharing bonuses happen, their personal self-interest is lined up with the company's self-interest. That is, employees drive to get their bonus by driving the main gainsharing formula items, which, in turn, drives company performance and profits.

The company and employees are in this together.

Meshing the employee's self-interest with the interest of the company directly addresses the usual mismatch of company and employee motivations.

When we set the gainsharing formula up so gainsharing performance tracks with profits and, at the same time, drives employees' bonuses, employees and the company are pulling in the same direction. Both are watching and driving the same measures, and they are literally working together towards the same goals.

This changes everything.

SUMMARY

A bonus is not enough.

Sometimes, management mistakenly believes if they simply set up an employee bonus system, employees will figure out how to drive results to get their bonus.

It's not enough to have a bunch of highly motivated, energized employees. They can see problems all over the company, but they don't always have the decision-making and implementation authority to fix the problems, make the decisions, and drive the gains.

Management people can be motivated by a potential bonus because they have the resources to earn that bonus. In other words, they can put a plan in place, make sure it's executed well, get feedback, make adjustments, and then earn the bonus.

But rank-and-file employees typically don't have the same information and resources to connect the dots and put the cause-and-effect in place to get from the first step of striving toward a potential bonus to making it a reality.

Rank-and-file employees depend on management to put the other pieces in place or make these resources accessible.

That's where the gainsharing process comes in. It provides the missing enabling elements. Employees are now not only motivated by a bonus, but they can put the pieces in place to earn that bonus.

Again, just offering a bonus isn't enough.

If we want employees to be motivated, we need to show them how to get what they want—what to do first and what to do next. They also need feedback to adjust what they're doing in real time. And finally, they need to actually get the bonus.

NEXT UP: HOW THE NEEDED PRODUCTION PLAN GETS EVERYONE PULLING IN THE SAME DIRECTION AND DRIVING SUCCESS.

Needed Production

"You can't hit a target you cannot see,
and you cannot see a target you do not have."

Zig Ziglar,
author and salesman

IN A CAUSE-AND-EFFECT world, we need to put the causes in place to create the results we want. If companies want employees to be motivated, accountable, and goal-focused, they need to provide the tools and work environment to make that happen.

Creating the plan in advance requires action. Without it, it's not possible to create motivation, focus, and accountability. This seems obvious. But many companies don't do this, and they wonder why their people aren't motivated or focused and are just putting in enough effort to get by.

The Needed Production Plan (NPP) spells out what needs to be done so that employees can earn their gainsharing bonus, both in the big picture and at the granular level.

It puts must-have pieces in place to create motivation, focus, and accountability.

NPP BASICS

The gainsharing formula provides a framework to calculate how things need to come together to earn a gainsharing bonus. For example, if we're going to have a terrific month, what does that look like? In other words, "What's the target?"

We can calculate what's needed using the gainsharing formula. How would we do that?

We start from the big-picture plan for the week or month and calculate the costs we can afford and desired outcome targets based on the work to be done.

Let's take one week as an example:

- What is the overall value of targeted short-term production?
- What are the target material costs for that week?
- What are the target direct-labor costs for that week?
- What are the target indirect-labor costs for that week?

We end up with a plan that lays the framework for the following process: If we do this work, complete these jobs, and don't exceed these costs, it will result in this total production value or sales value. And that result will lead to a gainsharing bonus.

THREE LEVELS OF INVOLVEMENT

In the Needed Production Plan, these levels include involvement, buy-in, and planning.

- **Top level:** Management puts together the plan to get a gainsharing bonus in the big picture.

- **Intermediate level:** Managers or area leaders approve and buy into their piece of the overall plan.
- **Frontline-worker level:** Frontline workers buy into their portion of the plan numbers as achievable, use real-time performance feedback info, and execute the work from start to completion.

Aaron Sage of Sage Oil Vac explains how this works at his company:

I tried to make my own plan in the past [before gain-sharing], but it wasn't tied close enough to what they were doing on a weekly basis or a day-to-day, weekly, or monthly basis. I had this quarterly formula that I made up. It was tied to tenure and what our profit was, and I had a percentage. It was not tied to what they [employees] were getting done at all. It was not tied to their day-to-day activities close enough. So the good thing about gainsharing is that it's more in their face, more in front of them [telling them] what they need to get done weekly.

We didn't have it before [gainsharing]. We didn't have a weekly production plan for those departments spelled out for everybody weekly. It was just, they would come in and ask, 'Hey, what do we need to get done?' And the production manager or the lead would give them a day's worth of stuff to get done. So they would get that done and then maybe that person would stall the next day for maybe half the day. And then they would come to them and go, oh yeah, I got that thing done. What's next for me?

This [gainsharing] is more like this is what we need to get done in the next seven working days. It gives more direction right down to the hourly wage person what we're trying to get done. And so I think that you just inherently, you're just gonna get more production. You're gonna get more value done because the production plan is more in their daily vocabulary than it was before.

Sage explains how the NPP is broken down and communicated at all levels of his company:

> Yeah, I mean we had it, we had a production plan [before gainsharing], but it was at the leadership team level, and it was on a quarterly basis. What [gainsharing] forced us to do is say, "Okay, here's our quarterly production plan. What does it look like monthly? Well, we need to get this much done per month. Okay. If we're gonna get this much done per month, what do we have to do weekly? Well, we have to get all this done this week, and it's made what we need to get done more granular.

It's important the NPP is communicated to all levels of the company.

As Sage explains:

> Previous [to gainsharing], Phil, our production manager, was trying to get across [to employees] what they needed to do weekly or monthly. And he was toying with different ideas on how to get the production schedule communicated to them in an effective way. And I think [gainsharing] . . . put numbers behind it. And that was something that he was looking for, a way to communicate down to the shop what he wanted them to get done. And that, in turn, made our shop leads understand how to communicate to their guys, down to how many parts needed to be done. So I think it gave them and it gave us an avenue or the thing to follow to get that communicated.

Getting everyone on the same page is essential. And the NPP makes that happen. Here's why.

FAILING TO PLAN IS PLANNING TO FAIL

When employees come to a gainsharing meeting, they want to know two things:

- Whether it looks like they're going to get a bonus
- What they need to do today to actually get a bonus

Management and employees shouldn't just muddle through the week and pull the numbers together afterward to see how the gainsharing results turn out. Without a plan, that's what you're doing. Essentially, failing to plan is planning to fail.

Management needs to be confident that when employees achieve bonus-level performance that employees will actually get the bonus. We certainly don't want management telling employees what they need to do to get a bonus, employees then do it, but they do not end up getting their bonus.

To walk the talk, management must put together a proactive plan that outlines and defines bonus-level performance. This plan works things through to ensure all the dots are connected so that when employees achieve bonus-level performance, they get their bonus.

Chupp of Woodenware puts it this way: "If [the NPP] forces you to do deep thinking, then that's what it does. It forces you to do deep thinking."

Just muddling through the week willy-nilly and things do not result in a bonus is completely unacceptable and a management failure.

Calculate Needed Production

The performance needed to pay a bonus with a set of costs is a straightforward, mathematical calculation. You calculate it using your company's information and gainsharing formula.

Start by calculating what constitutes good production. That is, if you were going to have a terrific month or week, what would that look like? What would the details of that performance be? Not calculating what needs to be done, doesn't change its reality. It is what it is.

FAILING TO PLAN IS PLANNING TO FAIL.

You're better off knowing what it is and encouraging everyone in your company to beat their goals for the hour, day, week, and month.

Well-known marketing expert Gary Halbert would tell all his clients, "You're in the arithmetic business. If your arithmetic doesn't add up, you won't have a business for very long. Start counting."[5]

Knowing your numbers and beating your numbers is essential to business success, no matter what business you're in.

The Needed Production concept addresses this reality directly. A plan to reach this target focuses on calculating these numbers and breaking this information down so people can clearly see what they need to do to achieve success and get a bonus.

As Aaron Sage notes:

> "I guess [what's] happening now [with gainsharing] that wasn't happening before is [that] all the leads and their people . . . think of their week in terms of the gainshare. They think of their week in terms of what the plan is and accomplishing the plan, and they know now the consequences of not reaching that plan because there's a number tied to it."

Some of you are probably thinking you can't lay out what each department needs to do each day or each hour because your company doesn't have the information you need to do that.

The question is: What information do you lack? "Do not let what you cannot do interfere with what you can do," says champion basketball coach and leadership guru John Wooden.

---

[5] https://www.thegaryhalbertletter.com/newsletters/zfzs_pearls_of_wisdom.htm.

How close can you get to that goal with what you have right now? Once you get started, you can continue by getting the other pieces in place you believe would be helpful.

The Needed Production Plan serves many purposes, and we will discuss those now in detail.

FIRST: THE NPP PROVIDES AN OVERALL PLAN THAT CAN BE BROKEN DOWN INTO COMPONENT PARTS

Let's look at an example of an NPP.

Using the formula, this is what the setup might look like:

- Overall production or sales volume needed
- Total material cost that could be allowed
- Total scrap rate allowed
- Total labor costs allowed (direct and other)

1.	Scheduled Production	200,000
2.	Outside Services	10,000
3.	Freight	8,000
4.	Scrap/Rework	3,400
5.	Value Producted	178,600
6.	Threshold	40%
7.	Target People Cost	71,440
8.	Direct Labor	18,000
9.	Indirect Labor	14,000
10.	Salaries	20,000
11.	Benefits	15,600
12.	Total People Cost	67,600
13.	Projected Bonus	3,840

FIGURE 13: *Needed production*

From the formula calculation using a specified sales value of scheduled production, we can calculate the costs we can afford.

For example in Figure 13, line 1 shows 200,000 in scheduled production. Lines 2, 3, and 4 show expenses to be subtracted from Line 1.

Line 5 shows value produced, which is line 1 less lines 2, 3, and 4.

The value produced is multiplied by the threshold percentage (Line 6) to calculate the total people costs we can afford.

Line 12 shows the total planned people costs.

Line 13 shows the projected bonus, which is Line 7 less Line 12.

So in Figure 13, we see $200,000 is scheduled. Following the value-produced formula with the expenses outlined, a bonus is projected in line 13.

Area accountability

Once the NPP is calculated, it can be broken down so that the people in each area or department can see what they need to do as their part in achieving the overall goal.

We want to calculate in advance what that big picture looks like. Then we want to break it down so we can communicate to the employees in each area their part of this big picture. In other words, this gives us the numbers they need to hit for this total plan to come together and generate a bonus for them.

If we don't calculate the overall goal, obviously we can't break it down. And if we don't break down the overall goal into its component parts, we can't hold the departments and areas accountable.

It may seem obvious that we need to calculate the overall NPP in advance, but most companies don't do it.

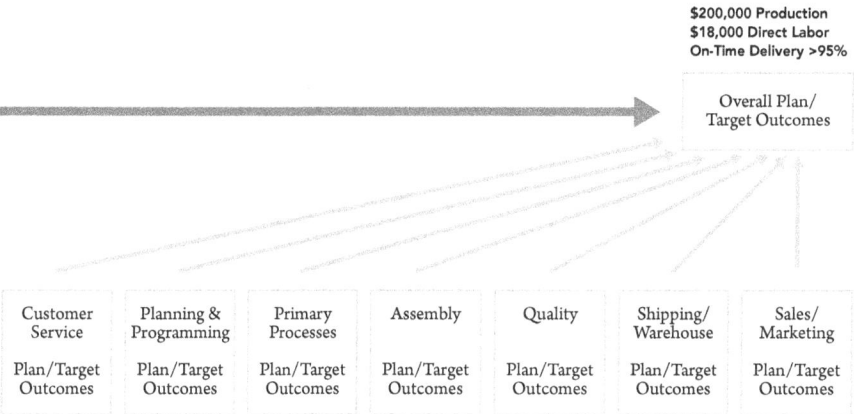

FIGURE 14: *Breakdown of plan.*

In Figure 14, we show a plan for a week that has $200,000 in production costs, $18,000 in direct labor costs, and on-time delivery of 95% or higher.

If we're going to achieve this plan, then all departments, all the different pieces of the company need to do their part. Whatever doesn't get done or is done badly affects the entire company like one fallen domino causing a cascading effect.

If we get to the end of the week and we haven't achieved the plan, then we should be able to go back through the departments and see where the shortfall occurred.

> "YOU'RE IN THE ARITHMETIC BUSINESS. IF YOUR ARITHMETIC DOESN'T ADD UP, YOU WON'T HAVE A BUSINESS FOR VERY LONG. START COUNTING."
>
> —GARY HALBERT

For example, if the total production was only $185,000, then we should be able to see which $15,000 in orders weren't completed. And we would be able to see where the wheels fell off, so to speak.

Let's say, for example, $15,000 worth of orders weren't completed in assembly because they were waiting for components that were behind schedule. But these components should have been completed in the primary processes. In short, the assembly department couldn't adhere to the schedule because they were waiting for parts they didn't have.

So now we can go through the specific cause-and-effect analysis to look at why these parts got held up in the primary processes and didn't make it through to assembly in order to complete the schedule for the week.

The proactive plan

Having an NPP in place allows you to calculate how things should come together to achieve a positive gainsharing result, or bonus, using the work scheduled.

Steve Hicks of Dongan Electric explains:

> Well, [the Needed Production Plan] didn't exist before [gainsharing]. You know, you had a series of orders sitting in the queue to make—let's make this one and this one. But I'm not sure [anything] was ever laid out ahead of time that broke it down to the individual person.
>
> That is to say, you've got a department of five winders [who wind electrical coils]. OK, who is person 1, 2, 3, 4, 5? What are they going to be doing today, the next day, and the remainder of the week so that they know what they need. And then, of course, the measure at the end of the week is how well did we perform against what we targeted them to build? Right. And then you add on multiple departments that follow on. So now you wound it, now you have to finish it, now you have to build it, now you have to assemble it.
>
> The advantage of knowing what's coming through the pipeline is a big deal. Because if you don't, the people down the line don't know what's coming to them. You know, it's kind of like they're downstream, but they don't know what's floating down the river. Now [after gainsharing], they do. And they can plan for it in

"DO NOT LET WHAT YOU CANNOT DO INTERFERE WITH WHAT YOU CAN DO."

—JOHN WOODEN

terms of making enclosures and getting leads available. And a lot of different little operations that nobody really sees. If you lay out what somebody needs to do, they have a far better probability of making that happen.

SECOND: ESTABLISH OBJECTIVES, THE MUST-HAVE PREREQUISITE FOR ACCOUNTABILITY

The NPP becomes the goal. Without the plan, there isn't anything to be held accountable to.

Without a goal or a plan, you can't have accountability.

Managers talk about wanting greater accountability. But you need to do the front-end work and set up the objectives. You need to set out the goals or standards that people will be held accountable to. You can't build in accountability after the fact.

This means that having the NPP on the front end is essential for accountability.

The overall Needed Production is, of course, the result of the performance of all the pieces. Combined, they form the big pcture. Look at the overall result needed, then specify what each department needs to do as its part in achieving the total outcome.

When the week ends, look back and see what people or department didn't achieve the targeted performance and, if this happens, identify where the gaps were.

At the end of the period, whether it's an hour, day, week, or month, we're accountable to the plan. The Needed Production Plan provides a comparison point and an objective comparison target.

How did you do in terms of your plan?

- Did you hit your number?
- Did you beat your number?
- Did you fall short of your number?

The point is, if you don't have the plan as a point of comparison, then it's not clear how successful the performance was. But once you have the plan, there's an objective target to be held accountable to and compared to. Without this comparison point, there can be no accountability.

The plan simplifies the challenge.

The objective comparison point the NPP provides is a must-have. It is what reveals where things are on track and where they're not.

Let's say, for example, that there is a small work group that has a goal of completing ten things. Let's also say that, in the end, the group was able to accomplish eight of the things and had problems with two. Being able to focus on those two issues, really simplifies the challenge.

To improve performance, we just need to address the problems with those two items. This allows us to focus and simplifies what's needed to improve performance.

Winners want to be accountable.

A winner wants to be accountable and to be held accountable. A winner wants to win.

And if you don't give winners a challenge to struggle with or obstacles to overcome, and you can show the kind of workers they are, they'll go where they can get those things. If there's no score, there's no winning.

This Needed Production process sets up the goals they crave and the feedback to hold them accountable.

THIRD: THINK THINGS THROUGH IN ADVANCE

Creating a weekly NPP demands that things are thought through in advance.

Find problems.

By involving managers in the development of the NPP, you'll discover and avoid problems before the problems occur. You won't need to wait until the plan is underway to discover the problems are there.

> **"SHOW ME A GOOD LOSER, AND I'LL SHOW YOU A LOSER."**
> —VINCE LOMBARDI

Of course, it's better to bring these problems to the surface to make adjustments up front.

Plan enough work.

Proactive planning allows us to make sure we're planning enough work to get a bonus and beat the profit goal.

If we don't have enough work scheduled to put together a bonus-winning plan, creating the NPP in advance brings this to our attention.

If we don't have enough work scheduled, is there work we could pull into the schedule that legitimately needs to be done, in other words, work you have orders for and the like. We don't want to pull in work that will just increase unneeded work in process or finished-goods inventory.

If we don't have additional work to pull into the schedule, perhaps we can adjust costs, such as overtime, to match the scheduled work.

Fix bottlenecks and other process problems.

Putting the plan together in advance reveals bottlenecks or other process problems before the week begins.

If there is a bottleneck in your process, you'll find out. Bottlenecks are likely already there. You just aren't aware of them. They're hiding.

By the time you're aware of them, you're stuck in reactive mode, dealing with the chaos, distraction, and crises they cause.

Creating your NPP in advance reveals the bottlenecks, and you can make changes to completely avoid them. The key here is knowing in advance these bottlenecks are going to occur.

Without creating the NPP, you're just muddling through by being reactive. You're fighting fires instead of preventing them.

FOURTH: MANAGEMENT'S PROACTIVE BUY-IN

Let's set the stage. We need to get managers to buy in and personally commit to achieving their part of the NPP.

When a manager buys into the NPP in advance, they:

- Approve and agree to the overall Needed Production Plan,
- Agree their part of the plan is reasonable and achievable, and
- Agree they can achieve their part of the total plan.

> **"THINKING IS THE HARDEST WORK THERE IS, WHICH IS THE PROBABLE REASON WHY SO FEW ENGAGE IN IT."**
>
> **—HENRY FORD**

In doing so, they're making a personal commitment—not only to their peers but to themselves. They're now personally on the line to follow through and be successful. If they don't make a personal commitment, they're literally not in the game. They're a spectator.

Without this personal commitment, there isn't the same sense of urgency as when they say, "I see the big picture. I see my part in that big picture. I can and I will do my part."

Getting a personal buy-in has huge motivational and leadership implications for the managers and the people they manage. It's a must-have.

FIFTH: EXPECTED OBJECTIONS TO CREATING A PLAN

There are predictable objections that you should anticipate regarding the development of an NPP. Some of the most common:

"The plan will need to be modified as soon as it's created."

Clients often say to me, "I can put a plan together, but it'll need to be changed shortly after the plan's created." This is true for most companies.

OK, how much of the plan will change? All of it? Probably not. Let's imagine 10% to 20% of the plan will change. Even if that much changes, the other 80% to 90% doesn't change.

As a result, you can get squared away on what it takes to get that 80% to 90% of the work done, which puts you in a better position to address the part of the plan that does change.

The point is only part of a plan changes, not everything.

"Creating the plan requires difficult thinking."

It takes difficult thinking to put a plan together. And that can stir resistance. It's so much easier to just muddle along and react to problems as they come up. Thinking is paramount; don't shy away from it if it's difficult. Remember Henry Ford's words: "Thinking is the hardest work there is, which is the probable reason why so few engage in it."

Most of the plan's value, though, is in the process of planning, not the plan itself.

Creating the plan, of course, requires thinking through:

- The performance needed,
- The costs the company can afford, and
- How the company is going to get the overall outcome management wants.

If there is no plan, if you haven't thought through what you want to achieve or what excellent performance looks like, you're just trudging along aimlessly.

Are you hoping that if you hustle and work hard, you'll somehow end up being successful?

"Some employees don't want to be accountable."

A second source of expected resistance is people who don't want to be accountable. They know the comparison point the plan provides can be used to hold them accountable.

But as managers, we must create an environment with objective accountability. Without the plan, there aren't specifics to hold people accountable to.

When someone is held accountable:

- They need to plan and think through the results they want to achieve.
- They have to address problems they couldn't or didn't anticipate.
- Their performance is visible, which they may prefer to avoid.

Being held accountable is more difficult than just showing up, putting in some effort, and leaving it at that. In many cases, people will avoid being accountable if they can get away with it.

And as we all know, effort isn't the same thing as achieving results.

"If we can't hit the plan, why bother putting it together?"

Sometimes, we're in a situation where reaching the Needed Production goal isn't possible.

I believe we might as well calculate the needed performance to achieve bonus-level performance and to exceed targeted profit levels, even if we don't know how to perform at that level right now.

The performance needed is what it is, a mathematical reality that can be calculated.

And even if the performance needed is not something we can do at the moment, if we calculate what it is, we can begin moving in that direction. We can show progress as we improve on our way to achieving the goal.

So if the goal is unachievable at the moment, that doesn't mean we shouldn't talk about what it is or that it's disheartening or will ruin people's spirit to calculate it. We can show our progress as we move towards the goal we need to achieve.

Once the needed performance is calculated, we can put together an action plan to do what can be done right now. This can allow us to create a kind of divide-and-conquer approach, where we're coming at the goal with efforts, strategies, and tactics that are achievable, in other words, something we can accomplish right now.

The progress we make increases momentum toward getting things moving in the direction we want to be going.

SUMMARY

The Needed Production process outlines the overall needed performance, which is then broken down into the component parts for each department to achieve its part of total performance.

To create the NPP, management must think through and outline the specifics of bonus-level performance. This overall specific performance can then be broken down into the needed departmental performance.

These specifics allow managers and departments to be held accountable to achieving their part of the specified performance. This lays the foundation for accountability and makes the gap visible between targeted and actual performance, which drives development of the fix.

In addition, the Needed Production process allows departments to see when their department misses their performance targets. This, in turn, affects other department's ability to hit their targets. The process lays the groundwork for the departments to problem-solve and work together more effectively, thanks to the specifics, visibility, and accountability it provides.

NEXT UP: WE PUT THE PIECES IN PLACE TO CREATE ACCOUNTABILITY, COMMUNICATION, AND PROBLEM-SOLVING.

7

The Script Meeting

> "Only three things happen naturally in organizations: friction, confusion, and underperformance. Everything else requires leadership."
>
> Peter Drucker,
> seminal management consultant and author

THE SCRIPT PROCESS is a centerpiece of gainsharing. The Script meeting is where employees make things happen. The Script itself is a compilation of information put together by various areas and departments. Each area prepares a couple panels following an established format. The information is usually pulled together into a presentation slide deck.

Without this process, your company is just going through the motions, and not deliberately driving the gains.

Tim Gase, President of Peerless Saw in Groveport, Ohio, once told me: "I like the Script process because it forces my management team to get together each week and discuss what was supposed to happen and what actually happened, whether they feel like it or have time for it or not."

It's called the Script meeting because it's where the content for the employee gainsharing meetings or communications is created. The content of the gainsharing Script is created so it can be presented like the script of a news program that the presenter reads.

That is, there's sufficient detail so the script content can be presented by anyone. This way, different presenters in different departments, on different shifts are all presenting the same message and information.

It also provides a deadline for the preparation of the plan for the upcoming week and a performance analysis of the week just completed, including fixes for the gaps between targeted and achieved performance.

Thanks to this process, a discipline is established for plan development, problem-solving, accountability, and communication.

As Aaron Sage notes: "The Script meeting has brought all the managers and the leads together. It's been the communication forum that we never had before. What comes out of it is good, consistent communication."

Each week, the Script group quickly reviews, discusses, and edits the information. It becomes a very powerful thirty minutes or so, where company leaders quickly see:

- How they did in reaching the goals,
- The problems they had, and
- The fixes that were started or put in place to address the problems.

A SCRIPT CREATES ACCOUNTABILITY TO THE PLAN

The emphasis here is on creating accountability, that is, deliberately putting the conditions in place that establish accountability.

Just having an Needed Production Plan doesn't ensure:

- Visibility or awareness of the plan,
- Comparison of plan performance to actual performance,
- Accountability for results, and
- The sense of urgency to fix performance gaps.

In the Script meeting each week with their peers present, leaders are held publicly accountable to performance on their part of the plan. If a company doesn't have Script meetings, they're missing a powerful, must have tool to create accountability.

The Script meeting content reveals whether a given department hit its numbers and its goals or didn't. The script information is objective. It's not somebody's opinion, and there's nowhere to hide.

This visibility builds and enforces accountability because each area is held accountable to its part of the total plan. And peers will get tired of hearing excuses week after week.

The weekly Script meeting routine also ensures the NPP is developed. Since the Needed Production Plan is reviewed in the Script meeting, this provides a deadline for the plan's creation and ensures structure and discipline in the process.

AND ACCOUNTABILITY TO BEAT THE PLAN AND EARN A BONUS

One of the most fundamental purposes of the Script meeting is to review the after-the-fact performance that was needed to achieve a gainsharing bonus.

The Needed Production Plan is broken down into what has to happen in the different departments, to roll up to the overall performance needed to be positive for gainsharing. The Script meeting provides a discipline for reviewing performance against the plan. Each week, all the relevant parties know their peers will be getting together and reviewing performance against their part of the plan.

This gives visible, objective accountability. This really speeds up the improvement process, as the "dog ate my homework' excuses quickly become apparent.

MAKES GAPS MORE VISIBLE, URGES ACCOUNTABILITY AND FIXES

It's not enough just to examine how we did against the plan. If the overall planned performance wasn't achieved, then one or more of the departments or areas must have missed their goal.

Since each department or area is accountable to achieve their planned performance, the script process gives visibility to these performance gaps, that is, where they missed their goal. If a department or area missed its goal, they're accountable to diagnose the problem and get a fix underway, so we don't have this problem again in the future.

Sometimes employees feel if they just explain why they missed their goal, they've done what they needed to do, and they're finished. But employees need to fix the cause-and-effect sequence that caused the problem in the first place.

If they don't put a fix in place, the same problem will arise again in the future. Having the Script meeting, where various departments review performance against targets throughout the company or facility ensures transparency, accountability, and follow through.

ENGRAINS THE DISCIPLINE TO APPROVE NEXT WEEK'S PLAN

In the Script meeting, we also quickly review and approve the plan for the upcoming week.

This is a very productive use of management time, as all the department heads are in attendance, and management can get a public buy-in to the plan.

GETS APPROVAL AND CONTENT CREATION FOR GAINSHARING MEETINGS, COMMUNICATIONS

The results of these discussions become content (the Script) that's reviewed and shared with everyone in the company in the weekly gainsharing meetings or communications.

At the end of the Script meeting, the management team agrees on the message that will be communicated throughout the company. This weekly routine of preparing the information for the Script meeting and then reviewing it together as a group provides a powerful communication tool, both within the group of department heads and throughout the company.

SCRIPT MEETING LOGISTICS

Who attends the Script meeting?

The Script group is made up of what I call the Heads of State. This typically includes someone from the major departments, for example, production, quality, material procurement, human resources, accounting, customer service, and sales or marketing, or both.

You may be able to have one person bring information from several smaller areas. For example, for production, you may just have the main production person in attendance. They can present information from several production areas.

A smaller group is better. If you can, limit it to four to eight people. That's a manageable group for the meeting.

Using technology, it's easy to include people into the Script meeting that are not on-site. They can get the script information, perhaps electronically. and quickly see, even though they aren't physically present, how things are going, problems that occurred, and solutions being put in place.

Who is in the Heads of State group?

You want to have different parts of the company able to contribute information, and to approve and contribute to the plan. The Script meeting provides an opportunity each week for issues to surface and action to be initiated on issues that aren't addressed in other company meetings.

The Script meeting provides an opportunity for the different parts of the company to be able to react to the Needed Production Plan, participate in the discussions, create buy-in on the analyses, and decide together on the strategy going forward.

Part of the intended dynamic for the Script meeting is to have the proper people in the room, to provide input from the various departments of the company, so you can't blame the results on the group that isn't included in the meeting.

If that happens, a department can't be scapegoated for performance problems because the group member that speaks for that department will be there to respond.

For example, someone can't blame or scapegoat maintenance by saying, "We missed our goal because of an equipment failure, when it really goes back to the equipment not working. My people can't hit the numbers if the equipment keeps failing. So not hitting the numbers is really an equipment issue, not my department's performance issue."

We want somebody in the room who can provide feedback from maintenance and react, perhaps by denying it was an equipment issue. That person may explain the production people didn't follow procedures and they ruined the tooling, meaning the equipment keeps failing because the operators did not follow specified procedures.

Being able to have this kind of discussion with the appropriate decision-makers present significantly speeds up problem-solving and the improvement process.

How frequently should Script meetings be held?

The Script meeting is typically held each week.

It's common for companies to still be making corrections in their hours reported and payroll information for the previous week on the following Monday. This payroll information is usually needed to complete the gainsharing report, which shows the results from the previous week.

Because of this, it's common for the Script meeting to be held on Tuesday or Wednesday.

How long should the Script Meeting last?

The gainsharing Script meeting generally lasts between 15 to 30 minutes.

To reduce meeting time, make sure the script information and content that needs to be reviewed is, of course, prepared in advance. This way, when the group gets together, they're quickly reviewing information, not putting the information together during the meeting.

In this half hour, you'll see:

- How you're doing against the plan,
- How you're fixing problems,
- Successes you've had, and
- The objectives going forward.

When the preparation work is done in advance, the meeting can move quickly, be informative, and be easily completed in a half hour or so. It becomes a powerful, effective meeting and an excellent use of a leader's time.

How much time does the Script process take each week?

Assembling the information for the Script process each week shouldn't take much more than 15 minutes or so for each of the areas that will be submitting information.

First, each area or department that submits information only has a couple presentation slide-deck panels to put together each week.

Second, they're placing information into an existing framework. This reduces the time needed each week to organize the information together.

And third, the preparation tasks are assigned to more than one person. So preparing the information and materials for the meeting becomes a task of many hands that doesn't overburden any individual.

There's an old saying that a teacher learns as much as their students. When the tasks of preparing, organizing, and presenting the information are shared among several people in an area or department, it creates involvement and understanding that you may not get otherwise.

It's essential to keeping the spark alive. You get different peoples' perspectives and inputs. It keeps the process continually evolving and adapting to the changing circumstances.

SCRIPT COMPONENTS

The gainsharing Script is assembled from presentation panels prepared by different areas of the company. A department or area may have one panel, or possibly several panels, that are incorporated into the final gainsharing script, which contains all the panels from the different departments.

It can seem like preparing a weekly gainsharing script involves an overwhelming amount of work. But it's divided among departments and becomes a many-hands task. A department or area may have one, two, maybe three panels that they prepare. These panels contain an overview or summary information the leaders of the contributing areas will know.

Also, the information for the panels is typically prepared and presented following an established format. This makes the meeting preparation process much easier and straightforward. Preparing a couple summary panels addressing the most important issues in their department, problems they're having, and the fixes they've put in place should not be difficult or take them a lot of time to create.

Let's go through a review of some of the common elements of a typical gainsharing Script.

Overview panel

It's meant to be a summary statement, kind of an opening for the employee gainsharing meetings where the presenter will cover the Script content with the employee attendees.

We want the same message conveyed at all the employee gainsharing meetings, so it's helpful for the Script group to come up with a common, agreed-upon condensation of the information to be reviewed.

It's common to cover:

- Whether they were positive for gainsharing for the week,
- Significant problems experienced, or
- New topics to be covered in greater detail in the Script content.

Actual vs. plan

Often, the next panel is a comparison of the actual performance in the week and the Needed Production Plan for the week.

It's good to have a single panel that looks at whether the group hit the plan target or not. This panel is intended to be simple, direct, straightforward.

Subsequent panels in the script information will detail the performance in different areas that, when combined, equal the overall performance.

Gainsharing report

The gainsharing report is like the scoreboard in a football game. It shows whether you're winning or losing but doesn't explain why. The panels and information that follow will get into the details of why the overall results for the week turned out the way they did.

Operations departments and areas

It's not enough to know whether the performance shown on the gainsharing report is good enough to be on track to pay a gainsharing bonus. We need to get into (1) what went right, (2) what went wrong, and (3) the fixes for the problems that kept us from hitting targeted performance.

Smaller companies might have just one section to address these topics. Larger companies may break the operations panels into several areas and departments.

It often works best to have this info presented in three separate panels:

- Comparison of plan vs. actual performance
- Rights
- Wrongs (and fixes)

Plan vs. actual comparison

If there is objective data available to show the planned performance versus the actual performance achieved, this can be very helpful. Objective data versus someone's opinion focuses the discussion and analysis on performance.

Objective information isn't always available. But if performance matters, measure it. If you can't measure it, it's hard to improve it.

What went right?

List or cover in some way three or four items regarding what went right during the week.

Sometimes it's difficult to find several things that went well and easier to find things that didn't go well. If we just report the things that didn't go well, employees feel these one-sided results feel a bit like a beat down and the good they do is not seen and appreciated.

This is a good place to give recognition and visibility to people or groups that did a terrific job during the week. Recognition is a huge motivator. Be sure to take this opportunity to showcase their terrific performance. We want to demonstrate the terrific performance will be recognized, made visible, and celebrated.

It can be effective to use employee names here to give employees credit and visibility.

What went wrong?

List three or four items that didn't go well.

Where possible, these items should spotlight the gap between planned performance and actual results.

Also, it's important that the fix for any problem be discussed. Otherwise, it's easy for a list of problems to become just a list of excuses for not hitting the goal.

It's demoralizing if we show we missed the plan targets and don't show whether there's anything being done to address the problem. Why should employees think future performance will be better if we don't fix the problems that kept them from missing the goal they were targeting?

Often, there are fixes and solutions underway. It's important to give these fixes visibility so people can see we're making changes; doing this helps avoid repeating the same problems again in the future.

Support departments and areas

Departments like maintenance, purchasing, quality, and shipping may also contribute a panel in the gainsharing script.

This format of having a panel for "What Went Right" and a second panel for "What Went Wrong" often is repeated for these support departments. Sometimes the format "rights and wrongs" doesn't work for the content of a department or area, and that's fine too.

Plan for upcoming week

What information do we have about the upcoming week?

Do you have 100% knowledge of the work scheduled for the week? It's helpful to let employees know the information you have, even if you only know, for example, 70% of the work you'll complete in the upcoming week.

You can get organized and be proactive about the 70% that you do know, which gives greater flexibility to respond to the additional 30% you're anticipating will come onto the schedule.

Are there any customer visits scheduled? Quality audits? It's good to get this info out.

A Needed Production Plan should already exist for the upcoming week that outlines the work, costs, etc. to be on track for bonus-level performance.

Including an overview of the Needed Production Plan for the coming week in the Script meeting gives a discipline and deadline for the plan's creation. The plan must be completed by then because the company decision-makers are expecting to discuss it as a group then, if they haven't already.

Including the Needed Production Plan in the Script meeting also helps fill in communication gaps. A given department may know about upcoming events in their own department; for example, maintenance probably knows about scheduled maintenance events. But this keeps the entire Script group informed about significant planned events throughout the company.

SUMMARY

The Script process is a crucial tool to drive productivity and accountability in a company. It involves weekly meetings where various departments provide information, which is compiled to be shared with employees throughout the company.

Script meetings serve several essential functions:

- **Create accountability:** The Script meeting ensures that the Needed Production Plan is not only created but also visible and comparable to actual performance. This visibility builds accountability.

- **Reviewing performance:** In the Script meeting, performance is compared to the plan, highlighting whether goals were met or missed. This drives urgency to address performance gaps.

- **Visibility of performance gaps:** If the overall planned performance isn't achieved, the Script process provides visibility to the areas that missed their goals. It ensures problems are given visibility and fixes implemented.

- **Approving plans:** The meetings also review and approve the Needed Production Plan for the upcoming week, establishing a deadline for plan development and ensuring a visible buy-in.

- **Content for gainsharing meetings:** The information discussed in the Script meetings becomes content for gain-sharing meetings or communications. This ensures consistent messaging and communication throughout the company.

The Script process fosters accountability and problem-solving, and ensures consistent communication throughout the company. It provides a way to get different parts of the company all on the same page and dramatically speeds up the improvement process.

To truly drive connection and motivation, we must connect to the day-to-day activities of employees.

Employees need to know what to do today to do their part toward getting their bonus and achieving the gainsharing goals.

NEXT UP: WE'LL EXPLORE HOW TO MAKE THIS CONNECTION AND DRIVE MOTIVATION.

The Boots-on-the-Ground Connection

THE BOOTS-ON-THE-GROUND CONNECTION is about having an individual worker know what they need to do on a given day in order to carry their weight toward achieving the bonus goal.

The engine of motivation lives in this Boots-on-the-Ground Connection.

It's not enough to know the overall performance needed to earn a gainsharing bonus. An employee needs to know specifically what they need to do as an individual to be doing their part to achieve the bonus goal. This connection gives a direct through-line connection between their daily work, getting a bonus, and the company beating its profit and other goals.

Companies struggle to put the Boots-on-the-Ground Connection in place. But it's a must-have for driving workplace performance.

THE BIGGEST MISTAKE

The biggest mistake companies make when trying to motivate employees is they speak in general terms when communicating goals and expectations.

A management-level person can work with either a general discussion of goals or the specifics. If you tell managers, "We have lots of work on the schedule, and if we really tear into this opportunity, we should have a good shot at a bonus," managers can translate that into what needs to be done. They can figure it out.

But the rank-and-file employee needs specifics.

If management tells employees there is plenty of work to do, employees may not know specifically what to do to earn their bonus. Employees need to know specifically what they should do so they feel they're doing their part. Thus, when management tells them the general plan and follows up with a specific outline of what needs to be done, employees want to get right to work. That's what they needed, and management just gave it to them.

More to the point, it helps to have the Needed Production broken down into something more granular.

Aaron Sage shows how this works:

> It just provides more accountability. I mean, it's more accountability down to each person on the team. That's what the granularity [aspect] does.
>
> [Maybe we say] the quarterly goal is that we need to ship 25 oil vac trailers in a quarter. Okay. What is that monthly? Well, let's see. So you got to get eight done in a month. Okay. Well, that means we have to get at least two done per week.
>
> And then you're going to the individual guy running the plasma [cutter] and tell him, "Guess what? You have to get

at least two done every week for this month. You have to plasma-cut two trailers a week."

And he's like, "Okay. That's the first time I've ever heard that!" [laughs]. That's fine. "Oh, okay. I didn't know I needed to get two done."

Then that [accountability also] goes to the person ordering the steel. We need at least two trailers worth of steel coming in every Tuesday, and before we weren't doing that. It was just, we were doing quarterly. [Now it's] we need to get this much done quarterly.

We were just expecting it all to happen. Well, the plasma operator, he may get one done and go, "Okay, I guess that's good. Is one good? I don't know if one's good."

And we were going, "How come we're not hitting our numbers?" [laughs] And then all of a sudden, we literally saw people on the floor, like, light up. They were, like, "Oh, I need to get this many tanks plumbed! I, I didn't know that! That's the first time you ever told me that!" You know, (we) were only walking out and saying, "Plumb these tanks. Here's how many. Here's the shop orders that I want you to work on right now."

But there was never a time frame . . . associated with it.

TO-DO LISTS

Spelling out the details, the specifics of what employees need to do to earn their bonus is like giving them a to-do list. Many managers use a to-do list or an organizer to plan their day.

If you've ever used a to-do list, does it:

* Help you be more productive?
* Help break down projects into steps to check off as you complete them?
* Help you see your progress?

- Give you a feeling of accomplishment as you complete the items?
- Make you more effective?
- Work for you?
- Do you think this would work for your employees, too?

We use to-do lists because they work.

Taking the Needed Production process down to the specifics, at the rank-and-file employee level, gives a to-do list to everybody in the company.

It will work for them to drive their performance, in the same way your to-do list works for you.

Completing items on your to-do list is rewarding. When you complete an item on your to-do list, it triggers in the brain a burst of dopamine, which is a neurotransmitter produced by the brain that can trigger emotions, such as pleasure, satisfaction, and motivation.

Says Earl Chupp, "You get your to-do list worked off, you got dopamine. When you complete a task and you write it off, [you get a hit of] dopamine in your body when you say, 'Complete.'"

Having clearly defined tasks outlined for the day, and progressively completing them allows workers to be more organized and focused, but it also gives them positive feelings, which motivates them to repeat this experience again in the future.

Communicating the specifics of an employee's target for the day can be done in many ways. For example, it could be that 1) certain jobs need to be finished, 2) certain tasks are finished, or 3) workers need to complete a certain number of standard hours of work. The key is being specific about what needs to be done.

You can start by working backward from the overall Needed Production performance for the week to spell out what employees need to do to be carrying their weight.

Be as specific as possible, down to, "These are the jobs or tasks or pieces that need to be completed by this time," and, "this is the allowed labor, material, and other specifics of the needed performance."

This contrasts with "do your best" goals, which are quite common in the workplace. With such general goals, employees just do all the work they can during their workday.

They may know which job to do first and which to do next, but nobody communicates clear, specific expectations about when and in what order something needs to be accomplished.

Employees want to know what they need to do today to be sure they're contributing towards the reaching bonus goals.

Do your employees know specifically what they need to do on their shift today to earn a bonus?

If they don't know, it's because they haven't been told. And it's up to management to tell them.

If they had been told, if they had been given this info, it would be on their mind and would make a difference in their performance, just as a to-do list makes a difference in your performance.

Having this boots-on-the-ground information can be a powerful motivator for employees jump into the fight to drive performance.

Employees can emerge as leaders with information they wouldn't have without gainsharing and the mechanisms it provides to speak up and drive performance.

> EMPLOYEES WANT TO KNOW WHAT THEY NEED TO DO TODAY TO BE SURE THEY'RE CONTRIBUTING TOWARDS THE REACHING BONUS GOALS.

Aaron Sage says:

> What we've seen on the floor is we've had leaders kind of just gravitate to the top because you start communicating to them in the weekly gainshare meetings, and it's motivating for them.
>
> When you start having the meeting with everybody in the company, what was shocking to me is people that you didn't expect any input from have stepped forward and said, "We're not gonna hit the numbers unless this stops happening, or we should do this if we really want to hit the numbers."
>
> And I think the leadership team is going, "Wow, this feedback that's coming from the lowest levels of our company is good."
>
> So what it has caused is leadership is coming from there, and people are getting promoted from those areas, because it gave them an avenue with which to speak up.

WHY THE BOOTS-ON-THE GROUND CONNECTION WORKS

It sparks motivation.

Motivation is a complex issue. But much of motivation at work can be boiled down to this: **People do what they do to get what they want.**

Telling employees specifically what they need to do to earn their bonus addresses this straight on. This sparks employee motivation in a way that pulls them forward.

As Grant Cardone says in his book *The 10X Rule,*[6] "Motivation isn't about getting all revved up and having something energize us

---

[6]   *The 10X Rule: The Only Difference Between Success and Failure*, Grant Cardone, 2011, John Wiley & Sons, Inc., Hoboken, New Jersey.

and push us. It's about what is necessary to have something to look forward to working towards that we're anticipating."

PEOPLE DO WHAT THEY DO, TO GET WHAT THEY WANT.

Feedback is essential to motivation.

To initiate and sustain motivation, it's essential that employees get feedback about progress towards their goals.

Anders Ericsson is a well-known expert on why some people are exceptionally good at what they do. He has studied musical prodigies, sports champions, and leading scientists to understand how they acquire their exceptional abilities.

In his book *Peak: How All of Us Can Achieve Extraordinary Things*[7] he notes:

> Generally speaking, meaningful positive feedback is one of the crucial factors in maintaining motivation. It can be internal feedback, such as the satisfaction of seeing yourself improve at something, or external feedback provided by others, but it makes a huge difference in whether a person will be able to maintain the consistent effort necessary to [achieve] purposeful practice.

It's also important that employees get information about how their job performance impacts other employees and departments.

Giving big-picture feedback shows employees that they're part of something bigger than themselves and that their impact on the overall performance is real, measurable, and quite visible.

---

[7]   Ericsson, A. & Pool, R., *Peak: How All of Us Can Achieve Extraordinary Things*, 2016, Vintage.

Jay Abraham, well-known marketing and business expert adds, "You can't be great unless everyone in your organization sees a connection between what they do and the outcome."[8]

In a cause-and-effect world, the performance of the pieces makes up the total performance. Individual employees' performance is an essential part of this overall performance. They are part of this big picture, and feedback from the boots-on the-ground connection shines a light on this reality.

Seeing their impact on overall performance is a must-have for motivation.

The Boots-on-the-Ground Connection gives them a through line, a direct answer to what they need to do today to be driving achievement of their department goals, company goals, bottom-line profits, and successfully achieving their company's business strategy.

Outlining this connection connects them to these bigger issues, connects them personally through their performance, and is a key element to giving their individual work meaning and driving their motivation.

Feedback improves performance.

If you're working and aren't getting feedback, you can't confirm you're on track and make adjustments to stay on track. We know from our own lives, when we're trying to make something happen, feedback helps us make adjustments and stay on track to accomplish what we're trying to achieve.

---

[8]   Jay Abraham, "Brian Kurtz, Jay Abraham, Mike Agugliaro at SBE June 2018," YouTube video, 1:02:56, July 19, 2018, https://www.youtube.com/watch?v=Zz--vWLbOCo.

Feedback and making adjustments are a necessary part of the process of making something happen.

This is true in sports and many other fields as well as in business.

Ericsson and Pool, say this about the need for feedback in *Peak:*

> "Generally speaking, no matter what you're trying to do, you need feedback to identify exactly where and how you are falling short. Without feedback—either from yourself or from outside observers—you cannot figure out what you need to improve on or how close you are to achieving your goals."

Employees may be in a fog.

When employees don't get feedback, it's similar to when a person is driving a car and suddenly drives into a fog bank.

In fog, there is, of course, less visual information and feedback. We can't tell where we are. And this creates uncertainty and anxiety. We can't tell if we're on track or drifting toward a crash.

When employees don't have clear goals and aren't getting feedback, it's like they're in that fog. What's the first thing most drivers do when they suddenly drive into a fog bank? They slow down. And they feel anxious and uncertain.

So when the fog suddenly clears as they're driving, what do they do? They relax a bit and probably speed up again. Why?

Because they're getting the feedback to stay on track and make adjustments. If management doesn't give employees clear goals and feedback, they're in a fog, they'll slow down, and they'll be anxious, stressed, and uncomfortable.

It's up to management to provide the information and feedback employees need to keep them out of the fog.

It transforms work into a game.

When employees drive results for their own reasons, there's less need to look over their shoulder to make sure they're staying on track. They do their best work because that's who they are, that's how they roll. This reduces the need to supervise or police employees.

As Mark Twain said, "Find a job you enjoy doing, and you will never have to work a day in your life."[9]

In short, the more we engineer work so employees drive results because they want to, the better it's going to be for both company and employees. It's going to work better for the company because employees will produce better results. But it will also work better for employees because their day-to-day, moment-to-moment work is more interesting, engaging, and rewarding.

If we set up employees' work like a game they're playing, they'll drive the results because:

- They want to,
- They find it fascinating, and
- The results are important to them personally.

WHAT CAN BE DONE TO MAKE WORK FEEL MORE LIKE A GAME?

Just as following a recipe leads to consistent, predictable results, you can deliberately, predictably increase employee motivation and engagement by building the following three essential elements into employees' work.

[9]   https://www.goodreads.com/quotes/646569-find-a-job-you-enjoy-doing-and-you-will-never.

Take action.

If something is going to be like a game you're playing, you must be taking action in some way.

There must be an objective, a goal, something that you're trying to do or achieve.

Get feedback.

You need feedback as you go through the day, week, month on how you're doing in relation to the goal.

As you get feedback and adjust your efforts based on the feedback, the work becomes more engaging.

This combination of taking action, getting feedback, and adjusting efforts based on specific feedback is what makes an activity into something like a game.

It must be something you want.

There must be something that you want, something that's important to you tied to being successful from the actions you're taking.

This keeps you striving and adjusting your actions and evaluating how you're doing to get what you want.

It can be something tangible, such as a bonus. Or it might be intangible, like surpassing previous performance.

When implementing a gainsharing system and meeting with employees for the program kickoff, I often go over these three points with the employees, and I start by asking, "Who here wants to make more money?"

I tell them, "We're going to outline what it takes each week to be on track for an average $200 bonus per person. Then we're going to break down what needs to happen in each of the areas as we go through the week so people can see if they're carrying their weight towards earning this bonus."

This addresses one point, having an objective; it gives the people something they're trying to accomplish. We're going to clarify for them what they need to do. We're going to define what good performance is, i.e., the kind of performance that will lead to a $200 bonus on average at the end of the month.

Then I tell them:

"We're going to give you feedback as you go through the week, as you go through your day, on how you're doing against your department's or area's goal. And, of course, we'll have problems. We will run out of material, certain people won't show up for work, but we still need to hit the number, and we'll do our best to find a way to do it.

"Then, as we focus on the performance and give feedback, performance will improve. And we'll see that it's really a matter of getting organized and staying organized, planning the work and working the plan, and we will hit the bonus performance goal.

"But it's not just about getting the bonus. It's about showing that you're pulling your weight towards the overall goal, that you're as good as or better than you were last year, last week. And that you're living up to your expected performance and your concept of yourself as an excellent performer.

"You're showing that that's true with objective measures."

Avoids entitlement.

Entitlement happens when people get something they want, and don't know what they did to get it. Because they don't know what they did to get the rewards, they expect to get them again in the future. Thus, they believe they're entitled. They don't see the cause and effect.

It's like snow falling in Minneapolis in the winter. It just happens.

The Needed Production Plan and Script process lay out what employees need to do to make performance happen and get bonuses. People see what needs to be done to get their bonus, that it's not automatic, not going to happen without them focusing and making it happen.

The Boots-on-the-Ground Connection gives real-time feedback showing whether they're on track to hit the goals they need to hit to get their bonus.

If people get a bonus and don't know what they did to achieve it, they'll expect it to just happen again in the future. This is the key to why they feel entitled. It also shows what needs to be done to avoid entitlement and proactively drive motivation.

To avoid entitlement, your employees need to:

* Know specifically what they need to do to earn a bonus,
* See how they are doing on achieving those things, and
* See that when they achieve those goals, they get their bonus.

This puts the employees in control. They know what to do to make bonuses happen. And they believe if they do what they understand they should do, they'll get their bonuses.

So it's not about being entitled. It's about taking action to make things happen, to make their bonus happen.

This feeling of control drives further motivation in the future. Because people see they're in control of getting what they want.

Employees getting boots-on-the-ground information is essential to making this causal connection, which drives future motivation. And it's up to management to make sure employees get this information so they understand the causal connection. Employees can't get this information on their own. Management needs to put the systems in place to give them this information. Without this information, this causal connection isn't established, and it's possible that entitlement will be established in the information vacuum.

So having boots-on-the-ground information not only drives future employee motivation, it also avoids entitlement.

SUMMARY

Employees need to know specifically how to be doing their part to earn their bonus.

Boots-on-the-ground information connects employees to the must-have essentials driving results.

It connects employees to:

- The overall Needed Production Plan,
- What they need to do to get a bonus,
- What they need to do today or right now,
- What their peers or other employees need from them.

This allows them to work with the specificity of a to-do list, which allows them to turn their work into a personal game. It also gives them the specificity they need to achieve their goals.

Because of this, they have the detailed information and feedback they need to spark and maintain their motivation.

We want to fix the problems, the barriers that keeps employees from beating their goals. If we don't fix the problems they encountered, we will encounter these problems again.

NEXT UP: WE'LL EXPLORE HOW TO INCORPORATE SYSTEMS TO FIND AND FIX THESE PROBLEMS.

9

Fixes

THE GAINS COME from the fixes, not the discussions, the thinking, the intentions, or the meetings. If there's no fix, all the discussions and explanations are a terrific waste of time.

It's all about the fix.

Why? Because it's a cause-and-effect world. If I intended to achieve a certain target regarding, say, the level of production, and I didn't achieve it, then there's a reason I missed my target. And if I don't make a change in the cause-and-effect sequence of things, I'm going to have this problem again.

So the gains really come from finding the necessary adjustments in our systems, in finding problems that need to be fixed and addressing a few of them each week.

For each of these problems, we want a fix that specifies who's going to do what, by when so we don't have to rehash the same problems again and again.

Much like someone using sandpaper to smooth out bumps on a surface, once the problems are eliminated, they erupt again in the future.

In addition, it's common for companies to have a certain problem that's, in turn, causing a whole list of other problems. And once you drill down into and address this core problem, it becomes much easier to consistently achieve better performance.

It becomes easier to plan the work, and work the plan.

As Gary Hicks of Dongan Electric says: "It's all about the fixes. The John Wooden philosophy [expressed in the quote at the beginning of this chapter] is a big deal and you just have to embrace that. And you have to embrace it at the management level. You gotta embrace it at the supervisory level."

SWEAT HARDER

When a gainsharing system is implemented, employees often expect it's going to be a "sweat harder, move faster," system.

Employees often think that the company doesn't appreciate what they do, how hard they work, and everything they do for the company. They fear that management now wants employees to do even more.

But we can only work so hard. There's a limit to how hard we can work. And even if we can withstand an outrageous level of effort, we can't work like that all the time. That's not sustainable; it's limited.

But there's no limit to how much we can improve our systems.

The gains really come from improving our systems. That is, they come from finding and fixing a few things each week that are taking us off track or causing problems. Once we put fixes in place, we don't have to address those problems again. If each week we find a few of these items and eliminate them, it becomes easier to achieve better results, possibly with even less effort than it took before.

As Earl Chupp says, "Changing the small little stuff is what makes you win. It's not the big stuff, it's the small little tweaks here and there and over here and over there. Oh, now the rubber's hitting the road. The big gains come from the little stuff."

For example, a recreational vehicle manufacturing company in Elkhart, Indiana, was conducting meetings to introduce a gainsharing program to all three of its plant shifts. The same issue kept coming up in meeting after meeting.

The employees at the meetings told me, "We don't have the material we need to produce to the schedule. When we go to get the material from storage, the material is not there because somebody has taken pieces out of a bundle and didn't record it. And now, instead of having 20 pieces as the paperwork indicates I should have, I have 16 pieces. So now I have to figure out how I'm going to achieve this production without the specified material I need."

When this issue was addressed once they got gainsharing underway, it became much easier for the people to achieve their scheduled numbers. Once the people had the materials they needed, they could do an excellent job of producing to schedule.

A PLAN AS A COMPARISON POINT

The Needed Production Plan plays a critical role in driving the creation of fixes. Why? Without setting up the Needed Production Plan in advance, there isn't a target goal or comparison point to make the problems stand out. You can't clearly see where you've missed the plan, if you don't have the plan there in advance and, thus, have a point of comparison.

In a cause-and-effect world, something must change for performance to improve. But what needs to change? Being able to select where to focus improvement efforts is the key to making the changes that need to be made.

In short, if you don't know what to correct, you can't put corrections in place.

High-performance experts Ericsson and Pool mention something similar to this in their book, *Peak*. They note a study of student musicians trying to reduce the number of errors made while practicing a musical piece, which was the subject of a study conducted by Australian psychologists Gary McPherson and James Renwick.

Ericsson and Pool noted that, "All of the students had good attitudes and were motivated to improve, so McPherson and Renwick concluded that the differences among the students most likely lay, in large part, in how well the students were able to detect their mistakes[10]."

The student musicians' practice was more effective when they were better at detecting their mistakes because they could more effectively focus their improvement efforts. They didn't just keep repeating the errors as they practiced. They could focus their efforts on correcting the mistakes and then practice playing the music without errors.

How does this relate to the workplace? As with the student musicians' mistakes, workplace problems reveal where adjustments are

---

[10] Anders Ericsson & Robert Pool, p. 78.

needed. We can't fix a problem we can't see. So it's necessary to be able to identify problems in order to come up with the fixes.

This seems basic and fundamental but is often overlooked. When I worked as a car and motorcycle mechanic during my high school and college years, I learned that clearly understanding the problem I was trying to solve was critical to being a productive, effective mechanic.

As a mechanic, if I didn't understand the problem I was trying to solve, I was likely to do a huge amount of work taking the machine apart, making some change, then putting it all back together, just to find that I still had the problem I was trying to solve. The more experienced mechanics taught me the most effective strategy is to invest time upfront in diagnosing the problem before getting underway with the fix.

Spending time on the front end diagnosing and understanding the problem saves time and effort in the end. As carpet layers say, "Measure twice. Cut once."

Beyond the Needed Production Plan, the overall gainsharing process provides different tools, different avenues to drill down to the problem and a fix that will work.

Aaron Sage explains:

> I think it's given us a forum to debate the fixes, the necessary fixes, in a positive way. Sometimes you have a territorial thing going on.
>
> What happened before [gainsharing] was I thought I knew what the fix was as the CEO. Or the production manager thought he knew what the fix was. And so the production manager and I would argue and debate behind closed doors what the fix is.
>
> But when you get everyone, the whole team involved, I think the production manager and I realized that neither one of us had an idea, or we were wrong about what the fix was.

We realized after hearing back-and-forth discussions of what went right, what went wrong, that the fix was actually something else.

Yeah. And that came from the fabrication manager. Maybe it came from, you know, one of the welders.

And everybody goes, "Oh yeah. That is actually what's going on."

That's where the focus on the fix, and maybe our discussions, the production manager, and the CEO weren't specific enough. They were too high level. It's like, "Well, we're not getting enough out of Fab to meet the numbers. And it's Fab's fault."

Well, when you get down to, you know, the granular again, you have the actual Fab Team talking. The reason we can't meet the numbers is, "We don't have the drawings to us in time." On a weekly basis, you know, something very specific.

So you end up fixing the small stuff, which ends up being the fix for the big department.

NOT A COMPLAINER

Sometimes employees hesitate to mention problems because they don't want to be seen as a complainer. So instead of bringing up problems that need to be fixed, employees don't say anything. Problems multiply and the problem-solving process doesn't get started.

When problems get fixed and performance improves, employees who brought the problems to light and put fixes in place become heroes.

So before long, you've had a profound change from people who are afraid they'll be seen as whiners or complainers and instead realize that by fixing these problems they become a hero or, at a minimum, they get positive recognition.

This is a subtle but important cultural change that happens over time. Bringing out, highlighting problems is seen as a positive thing. The fear diminishes that you'll be seen as a complainer if you bring up a problem.

They're fixing the frustrating problems and helping everyone get bonuses. It's good all around.

FIXES MAKE TOMORROW BETTER

Sometimes employees feel that if they can explain why they missed their goal they've accounted for the gap, and they stop thinking about it.

But they need to push through to the fix. The fix is the reason tomorrow is going to be better. The fix is the reason the performance is going to be better because they're going to eliminate a problem that kept the team from hitting the goal. So the next time they're shooting for this goal, they won't have that problem. This is where the gains come from.

And it's not critical or essential that a fix work as soon as it's tried. If the fix doesn't work, adjustments can be made, and changes or additions made to refine the idea. When you try different options, you'll eventually find a way with to make the fix work.

It's important to emphasize this with employees because employees may be hesitant to speak up and are thinking they should keep quiet if they're not sure an idea will work.

As managers, people disagree with us frequently. Over time, we become less sensitive to this and forget other employees may be hesitant to speak up or bring their ideas forward.

So it's important that management work to create an environment where employees see that it's fine if their ideas don't work initially.

FIXES BECOMES A LIFE SKILL

Developing and implementing fixes educates employees about basic problem-solving skills, which is a capability useful to employees outside of the workplace. Many employees have not had basic problem-solving training. So getting experience with problem-solving in the workplace can lead to huge benefits in other areas of their life as well.

Earl Chupp of Woodenware says:

> I want tracking so people can see that they didn't get where they were targeting. All of this teaches employees how to think differently, set goals for themselves, stretch themselves and their performance, respond to feedback, pull together as a group, and stay pointed toward an overall result and a higher level of performance.
>
> This becomes a life skill where people see, "I can set a goal, I can set up feedback, I can work through problems, I can work together well with others towards being our best selves individually and together.
>
> We need more people stepping up and taking responsibility. Higher engagement level is often the difference between a good and a great company."
>
> All of this sets up a culture where people are comfortable taking responsibility. It puts together a framework where they can set themselves up for success in a step-by-step manner. People want to achieve, and this gives them the tools to set themselves up for success.

GREATER UNDERSTANDING FROM INVOLVEMENT

As employees are involved in solving problems in the business, they become more familiar with the basic problems and challenges their company faces. This greater direct involvement leads to a better understanding of business fundamentals.

In a 1958 book, *The Scanlon Plan: A Frontier in Labor-Management Cooperation*, Eldridge Puckett notes:

> A principle that is often overlooked yet one which can be most significant is the educational value of focusing attention on variables that are of critical importance to the firm. When there is an adverse shift in the product mix, or a decline in sales, or a competitive pricing problem, employees immediately feel the effects, attempt to isolate the reasons, and attempt to conquer the problem. Merely understanding the cause makes it easier to weather a rough storm—much easier than when the worker thought all the adversity started with a bum decision by management. Many companies spend tremendous sums today to educate their employees in the economics of the free-enterprise system. What better education can the workers get than by living, feeling, and working with the most basic problems of the particular enterprise they are a part of?[11]

---

[11]   Puckett, p. 73.

SUMMARY

The gains come from the fixes. The result of this is obstacles to attaining goals are removed, so it becomes easier to achieve and sustain improved performance. Identifying and fixing problems becomes visible and celebrated.

Because of this, the culture of the company is changed to promote focusing on objective performance data, identifying and fixing problems, and enthusiasm for continually feeding goals. It moves away from a culture where identifying problems leads employees to be seen as complainers. It makes it more likely that they will speak up and contribute to the improvement process. It makes the fixers, improvers, and heroes celebrated individuals.

NEXT UP: NOW WE'LL EXPLORE HOW TO DESIGN YOUR GAINSHARING SYSTEM AND GET THINGS UNDERWAY.

10

Design & Implementation

"In planning for battle, I have always found that plans are useless, but planning is indispensable."

Dwight D. Eisenhower,
34th President of the United States

TO GET GAINSHARING'S benefits underway, you need to design your gainsharing system to address your company's needs and characteristics.

No two companies are alike. So all gainsharing systems will be different, too. The gainsharing system must accommodate differences in management styles, different products or services, different employee needs, and the company size and structure.

This doesn't mean every detail of the gainsharing system must be created from scratch. It's a straightforward process of applying and adapting the basic concepts of the six-piece model outlined in this book.

These basic gainsharing concepts can be applied in many ways. And changing the specific ways they're implemented helps keep the system fresh and in tune with your company's circumstances.

THE DESIGN PROCESS

Designing a specific gainsharing system starts with 1) outlining what needs to be done, 2) how to achieve it, and then 3) how to make it easier to do or automate the task.

If you don't separate these steps, it's easy to get off track from what you want because you can't figure out how to do it.

Often in discussing options during the design process, if we can't figure out quickly how to do something, the discussion changes to doing something different. That is, the "what" gets changed because we can't figure out the "how."

But we don't want the discussion of how to do something to change what we want. Just be aware of this tendency. If we can get clear about what we want, we're very likely to figure out a way to do it, even if it takes a while to do so.

So let's go over some of the basic issues that often come up in design.

LOGISTICS

1. Get things started

It often works well to get the main people who will be involved in the design together at the beginning of the process to outline how the work will unfold.

This gives an overview so they know what to expect. You can also make it clear you will only be involving or calling upon the relevant people for the work at hand as it proceeds. This allows people to stay focused on their current obligations and become involved in the design as needed.

2. How often to meet

It's common for the design group to meet every week or every other week for a couple hours.

This gives the design team time to move forward with the other work they need to do and keep momentum moving on the design.

NUMBERS

The first part of the design is focused on formula development. So in the beginning, we often only need the numbers person or people, such as the CFO, controller, or accountant, and the main decision-maker, which often is the president.

1. Approve goals

Formula performance must demonstrate a win-win for both company and employees. To do this, it's important management is clear about the performance needed before they'd be comfortable paying a bonus.

I call this defining "What good looks like." That is, if the company was breakeven for profit, would management be comfortable paying a bonus? Probably not. Would the company need to achieve a profit that's 20% of sales before they would be comfortable paying a bonus? That's probably too much, too difficult. So the performance they're comfortable with is obviously somewhere in between.

Your formula is set up to drive the 80/20 performance levers, so higher performance is associated with better profits.

2. Formula simulations

When developing a formula, a key part of setting it up and demonstrating that it's working correctly is with simulations. One of the best ways to speed up the process is to begin simulations as soon as possible.

That is, you take your draft formula setup and simulate which months result in bonuses. This will allow you to quickly see any problems. The most recent 12 months often works well for these simulations. If you simulate which months you would've had a bonus, how much the bonus would be, and whether the payout seems appropriate considering the company performance in that month, you'll quickly see problems or other issues that need further attention.

You may find that one month shows a surprisingly large bonus compared to other months. As you dig into the details, you'll find what's driving the unexpectedly large bonus for the month—for instance, perhaps an inventory adjustment is needed. Once the issue is identified, you can decide how to address the issue and simulate again.

It's like sanding down the bumps or rough spots on a surface. Once you get the first set of bumps smoothed out, you may see another issue that you didn't see before. But using simulations this way will quickly call the important issues to your attention and save you a lot of time in getting your formula squared away.

3. Buy-in through participation

People support what they help create. Case in point: Employees who were involved in their company's formula development and testing process have told me it gave them a deeper understanding of their company's financials.

It took financial complexity and made it simple. They've told me it gave them a new understanding about which numbers really count. And they were then able to focus employees on these numbers or measures.

Management people who were involved in their company's formula design say, very quickly after gainsharing was implemented, the employees were asking insightful questions. These management people said they surprised themselves, in that they were able to answer these questions for the employees right then and there because the issues had come up during the design process. Their deeper, improved financial understanding during the design process occurred so gradually they hadn't been aware it was happening.

4. Driving company performance

Even if managers or decision-makers are not part of the gainsharing design efforts, it's important they understand that the gainsharing formula:

- Creates a win-win for company and employees, and
- Drives the financial and other outcomes they as leaders are charged to achieve.

Sometimes, before management understands what gainsharing is, they have a misperception that it's a giveaway system where bonuses are paid without regard to performance.

A management team is accountable to deliver results. They're evaluated on the results they achieve.

Even if they're not involved in the design process, it's important management understands that gainsharing drives the same performance and measures that they as management are accountable to achieve.

It brings everybody into alignment, pulling in the same direction.

5. Frequency of payout

The majority of gainsharing systems use a monthly gainsharing period. Longer periods (for example, quarterly gainsharing periods) can lead to a long delay between good performance and receiving a bonus. A weekly gainsharing period is typically too short to accommodate the swings in performance that happen in many companies from week to week. A monthly period allows a balance of week-to-week performance swings and still allows a timely connection between performance and reward (bonus).

Many companies using a monthly gainsharing period use what is called a 4-4-5 pattern, where one month has four weeks, a second month has four weeks, and a third month has five weeks. This 13-week period tracks closely with the three-month calendar quarter.

Sometimes, companies using the 4-4-5 pattern for their monthly gainsharing period will calculate the payout at the end of the month from the monthly financials. They prefer to calculate the payout for the final gainsharing results for the month from the month-end financials because they have confidence in those numbers once the financials for the month are closed.

They report the weekly gainsharing numbers to employees. And they make sure employees understand the weekly numbers represent the information the company has as the month progresses and are not the final numbers. The final numbers won't be known until the month-end financials are completed. But once the month-end numbers are closed, then the final gainsharing performance for the month is calculated from these month-end numbers.

At times, companies, especially larger companies, will argue for a quarterly payout. Often, this is because management thinks in terms of quarterly time periods.

But a calendar quarter is a long period of time for many rank-and-file employees. It's as though they should work hard during the summer because they might get a bonus in the fall.

The longer the delay between performance and rewards for that performance, the weaker the motivational power of that reward. So having a longer delay between good gainsharing performance and getting a gainsharing bonus for that performance weakens the motivational power of the gainsharing bonus.

There are circumstances where a quarterly bonus or a longer gainsharing period is necessary. But, if possible, a shorter gainsharing period is preferred

ELIGIBILITY

1. Who is included?

Regarding which employees should be eligible to receive gainsharing bonuses, the starting position is typically that all employees in good standing should be eligible.

Management will sometimes argue they shouldn't be eligible for gainsharing bonuses because it will reduce the bonus pool and hence the bonuses paid to other employees. The reality is that employees are reassured when they learn management is in the same boat, i.e., the same bonus system as they are.

Making management eligible for bonuses is considered during the design process and simulations. So it's not necessarily true that bonuses paid to other employees would be reduced because management is included in payouts, since they would also be included in the numbers used during the design.

2. For employees in good standing

I often include a provision that requires an employee to be "in good standing" to be eligible for the gainsharing bonus during the period when the bonus is paid.

This provision can help simplify calculating and distributing bonuses at the conclusion of a gainsharing period.

For example, if a new employee comes to work, just works a couple hours, and leaves never to return, the company doesn't need to find this employee who walked off the job to give them their small bonus for the couple of hours they worked. This also helps with employees who are fired.

3. Management already participates in a bonus system

Management may argue they already participate in a bonus system that's tied to company performance. So they shouldn't be eligible to receive gainsharing bonuses because it would be double dipping.

Gainsharing bonuses are provided in addition to employees' existing compensation. This is true for rank-and-file employees, and I would argue that it should also be the case for management.

A management employee may have compensation that's a combination of a base salary and a bonus tied to company performance or their individual performance. This is how the management person's pay is structured. It's their existing compensation.

And I posit that since gainsharing is additional compensation, over and above pay for the rank-and-file employees, it should also be additional pay for management employees.

4. Track together

If management participates in a separate bonus program, it's critical their bonus program tracks with gainsharing payouts and performance.

That is, the two bonus systems must not be in conflict.

As the old saying goes, "The man who chases two rabbits, catches neither."

People pay attention to what their pay is tied to. A management bonus system that isn't in harmony with gainsharing measures and bonuses, gives management conflicting goals.

When there's a separate management bonus system in addition to the gainsharing bonus system, be sure to test that the two systems are not in conflict.

It's not enough that it seems as though the two systems are not in conflict, or common sense would indicate that the two systems are not in conflict. Be sure to gather data and test through simulation whether the two systems perform together in harmony and are not in conflict.

NEEDED PRODUCTION

1. Needed production design and simulations

Once the formula design and simulations are completed, we move forward to the Needed Production process.

We take the numbers framework the formula provides and calculate with the current cost factors, including total labor costs, material costs, etc., what total production is needed to achieve an excellent week or month.

We are essentially defining what good looks like. It would be our desired target. That is, if we're going to have an excellent week or month with the current cost structure, for instance, labor costs, material costs, and margin favorability of scheduled work, what total production do we need to have an excellent week?

This is done at the big-picture 30,000-foot level.

We want to put together a plan that will have us on track to pay a gainsharing bonus. I usually target performance that would have a company on track to pay an average $200 per person bonus at the end of the monthly gainsharing period.

Once this overall plan defining what good looks like is put together, we can break this overall plan down into what must happen in the different areas for performance to roll up to the overall plan and performance we've outlined.

2. Get mid-level leaders involved

Often during the formula development and needed production calculations, the initial calculations are done with a small group of main decision-makers.

This way, we can have the necessary people moving the design work forward and maximizing the effectiveness of everyone's time.

It's been my experience that frontline leaders and middle managers would prefer to comment on or react to a draft of the design versus being involved from the beginning of the process designing the gainsharing system from the first step.

I often think about the initial gainsharing system design as a prototype. When I present it to the middle-level leaders, I discuss it that way, telling them, "Here are the questions we asked, and the answers we came up with. Do you agree with the way we put things together? What would you do differently? What should we add? What should we have asked that we didn't ask? How do we connect this to the Boots-on-the-Ground Connection level?"

Often, middle-level leaders are much more comfortable reacting to the proposed draft design in general terms, saying "I like this idea," or "I don't like that idea," versus starting at square one.

3. Breaking down the plan

Sometimes companies struggle with the question of how to break down the plan.

But I've never encountered a company that was absolutely at square one on this. They're taking care of business now. They have a way of laying out what has to be done overall, what needs to be done first, what needs to be done next, so that the products and services are completed on time and are what the customer wants.

So spelling out how this overall plan is broken down starts with going to the existing planning and scheduling information and using this information as your starting point.

The new production plan should define what needs to be finished in a certain week. But we must also define what needs to happen at each of the different stages in the process to keep things moving.

4. Marbles through the tube

I often think of the production process as a tube filled with marbles.

The first question is, "How many marbles do I need to pull out of the tube this week to be positive for gainsharing and on track to pay a bonus?" So I define that in terms of the specific jobs to be completed.

But then I also need to outline the marbles that need to continue to move through the tube so that we don't just empty out the end of the tube, have a great week, and thereby ruin the following week.

Note that this same discussion applies to providing services.

METHOD OF DISTRIBUTION

There are three main ways that companies distribute gainsharing bonuses: equal shares, per-hour bonus, percent of earnings.

1. Equal shares

The equal shares method divides the bonus pool to be distributed by the number of eligible employees, and each eligible employee receives the same dollar amount as their bonus payment.

This is conceptually simple. But this method gives the same dollar amount in bonus to a part-time worker who just started their job a month ago and only worked ten hours in the bonus month as it does to a long-term employee who worked a lot of overtime, is highly skilled, and can do multiple difficult and important jobs.

2. Per-hour bonus

The per-hour bonus distribution method divides the total bonus pool by the total number of hours worked. The bonus is then distributed according to the number of hours that an individual employee has worked during the gainsharing period.

Employees who have worked more hours would be paid a larger bonus. An employee's pay rate does not influence the bonus amount, only the number of hours the individual employee has worked.

3. Percent of earnings

The percent of earnings method divides the bonus pool to be distributed by the total gross earnings of all eligible employees including overtime. This resulting fraction gives a percentage that is used in distributing the bonus pool among the eligible employees. An individual employee's bonus is calculated by multiplying their gross earnings for the gainsharing period by the bonus percentage. This way, all employees receive the same percentage of their pay as a bonus.

The dollar amount of individual bonuses can vary where their gross earnings are different. But all employees still receive the same percentage of their pay as a bonus.

FAIR LABOR STANDARDS ACT

For companies in the United States, The Fair Labor Standards Act (FLSA) states that certain types of bonuses must be taken into consideration when calculating an employee's regular rate of pay when determining their overtime pay. The types of bonuses that must be taken into consideration when calculating overtime pay depend on their nature and purpose.

The **following types of bonuses** must be included in overtime pay calculations unless the bonuses are paid on a percentage of employees' total wages, which includes straight time and overtime:

- Attendance bonuses
- Piecework wages
- Individual or group production bonuses
- Bonuses paid for work done in less than established standard time
- Bonuses for quality and accuracy of work
- Bonuses paid as an incentive to attract employees

The FLSA states that if a bonus is calculated on a percentage of an employee's earnings, including straight time and overtime, no recomputation of the regular rate will be required for the purposes of calculating a worker's overtime rate. In effect, the percent of earnings method meets the legal requirements stated in the FLSA[12].

IMPLEMENTATION

Once you get the gainsharing system designed and ready to put in place, it's time to get the process underway. This is when the fun really begins.

Once employees see all the design work that's been done, how the design addresses problems and concerns they've had, and gives

---

[12]   Fair Labor Standards Act, Title 29 U.S. Code § 778.503, 1938.

them what they need to drive results, they'll be eager to get things started. Then it becomes a many-hands task and excitement grows.

Implementation of the design works like this:

1. Introduction meeting with employees

When it's time to introduce the gainsharing system to employees, sometimes companies get all employees together at one time. This way, all employees hear the same message at the same time.

If there are multiple shifts or other logistical difficulties that make it difficult for everyone to get together at the same time for introduction meetings, smaller group meetings can be held, and that works effectively as well.

This method has the advantage that sometimes employees are more comfortable asking questions in a smaller group versus a large group with 30, 50, or 200 people all together at the same place and time.

2. Training for holding gainsharing meetings

For many people, giving a presentation in front of a group can be terrifying.

Because of this, it makes sense to put together a training program to train people how to hold gainsharing meetings. This can give them a framework to follow and allow them to simulate holding meetings before they do so.

We want all the employee gainsharing meetings to follow the same consistent structure and present a unified message.

Because being in front of a group can be so difficult for many people, if we give them a structure and content to present, they can practice giving presentations and become more comfortable with doing so.

So before the gainsharing system is implemented, it's a good idea to get the people together who will be holding employee gainsharing meetings and go through a basic training program for holding the employee gainsharing meetings.

In this training, you will want to go through the content that they will be covering in the regular employee gainsharing meetings. This will allow them to get familiar with it and be prepared to answer questions.

You'll want to cover:

- Basic dos and don'ts for holding meetings
- How to prepare the meeting area
- How to start the meeting
- How to proceed through the presentation content
- How to finish up the meeting
- What you're likely to forget as a presenter
- How to handle difficult questions or situations that may come up

You will want to allow them to simulate holding a gainsharing meeting in front of the other presenters to practice the routines and get comfortable with holding gainsharing meetings.

At the end of this training, the presenters will be in good shape to hold effective gainsharing meetings and will be more comfortable in doing so.

SUMMARY

The gainsharing design process outlines how the six-part gainsharing process will be implemented at a particular company.

Every company is unique, and its gainsharing system must be designed to meet the company's specific needs and characteristics.

It's important to first get clear on 1) what you want in the design process. Once that is established, proceed to figuring out 2) how to do it. And then consider how to make the tasks 3) easier to do on a regular basis. Separating these steps is crucial to stay focused on the desired outcomes and avoid getting sidetracked by challenges in figuring out the how.

The design process usually begins with the formula and measurement issues, ensuring that driving gainsharing performance is a win-win for company and employees. The focus then shifts to clarifying what individual employees need to do to drive the formula and measurements in their daily tasks.

This aligns all employees with company goals and performance measures, and gets everyone on the same page, pulling in the same direction.

Once the design phase is complete, the implementation phase usually begins with meetings to introduce the gainsharing system to employees. This is typically followed by training sessions and regular gainsharing meetings and communications.

Each week, the company management and employees will review their performance against the plan for the week. As they put fixes in place to address performance gaps, company performance will improve, excitement will build, and eventually gainsharing bonuses will be paid.

It's truly exciting as employees see that they've made the gains happen. It gives a real sense of control that they can plan the work and work the plan, and that they work together in a way that brings out the best performance in each other and the company.

NEXT UP: WE'LL SUMMARIZE WHAT WE'VE LEARNED.

11

Be Bigger, Stronger, Better

**"That some achieve great success is proof
to all that others can achieve it as well."**

Abraham Lincoln

ONE OF THE most important, if not the most important reason to
have a gainsharing system is to make your company the bigger,
stronger animal in your marketplace. That is, make it more profitable
and better positioned to compete and grow, and attract, hire, and
retain the best employees.

Every company is a combination of the financial side and the
people side of the business. No other tool incorporates both of these
realities, ties them together, and drives performance to ever higher
levels like gainsharing. As Patrick Brandon, President of Contract
Medical Manufacturing told me, "Gainsharing is the glue that holds
it all together."

When a system is built to achieve something, it is much more
likely the intended outcome will occur. Gainsharing is a system to
drive financial results, and create and sustain motivation.

Having an ongoing system to drive these outcomes is like the
difference between a person working out in a gym and doing a

random sequence of exercises versus working out with a trainer, who supervises and challenges the person saying, "Is that all you've got today? Can't you give me just one more?"

LET'S SUMMARIZE WHAT YOU'VE LEARNED

- **Pay-for-performance**
  You've learned how to drive and reward performance. And you aren't stuck with just giving automatic pay increases as your only option, where you're paying employees more for the same performance.

  You've seen how gainsharing creates pay for performance, and it fixes the mismatch problem where management is trying to drive financial performance, but employees are paid for their time. This way, everyone is pulling towards the same goal and rewarded when they're successful.

- **Bonuses throughout the year**
  You've learned how to put together a system that doesn't just reward people at the end of the year. That is, gainsharing creates a system that rewards people throughout the year and generates real motivation, at the same time, driving company performance and profits.

You know a year-end bonus doesn't drive results or motivate employees. Now you've seen how to have a system that drives daily-weekly-monthly results and pays bonuses throughout the year. The feedback, measurements, and rewards drive, feed, support motivation all year long. It puts the fundamentals in place required for ongoing motivation.

- **Job shop**

You've seen how gainsharing can be done in a job-shop environment where you're producing small quantities and not doing repetitive work.

There are multiple formula options that work well in a job-shop environment. Putting together the Needed Production Plan, and Boots-on-the-Ground Connection is not a problem either.

- **Boots-on-the-Ground Connection**

You've seen how gainsharing makes it clear to individual employees what they need to do on a daily basis, to be doing their part toward achieving their gainsharing bonus.

This creates a direct, through-line connection to driving the bottom line. But it also gives the employees a daily to-do list that clarifies what they need to do today.

This clarity about what they need to do today, gives them focus, clear goals, feedback, and accountability that are essential to creating and maintaining motivation.

- **Complex to simple**

You've seen how gainsharing takes the overwhelming complexity of your business and makes it simple.

As Einstein said, "If you can't state it simply, you probably don't understand it yet."

Gainsharing gives your company a common language and focus. It's a flexible focus that adjusts with the challenge and allows the company to be nimble as it pursues the overall goal.

Distilling the complexity of business down to a common message brings everyone together on the same page. This makes teamwork possible.

- **No missing pieces**
  Now you know the six must-have pieces you need to have
  a complete system that will motivate your employees and
  make the motivation last.

This is a powerful, proven combination.

You could implement any of the six pieces by itself. But each piece adds momentum and effectiveness to the others. For example, it's not enough just to have a bonus system. If employees aren't focused on driving the factors that drive the bottom line, then the company could owe employees a bonus when the company was more profitable.

To have a long-lasting, successful system, it takes all six pieces.

Others have done this. You can do it, too

It's a cause-and-effect world. If you do what others have done, you can achieve the same success they have. But you have to take action.

> "THAT SOME ACHIEVE GREAT SUCCESS, IS PROOF TO ALL THAT OTHERS CAN ACHIEVE IT AS WELL."
>
> —ABRAHAM LINCOLN

Like many companies, you've already invested huge amounts in your equipment, facilities, and people. What we're talking about here is increasing the return on these investments you've already made.

But knowing what to do, and that others have been successful, is not enough.

To get results and the success others have, you need to take action.

Let the gains begin.

BIBLIOGRAPHY

Belcher, John G. Gain Sharing: the new path to profits and productivity. Houston: Gulf Publishing Company. 1991.

Bullock, R.J., "Gainsharing—A Successful Track Record," World of Work Report, Volume 9 Number 8, August 1984, p 3-4.

Bullock, R.J. and E.E. Lawler III, Gainsharing: A Few Questions and Fewer Answers, Human Resource Management 23, no. 1, (Spring 1984), 24-40.

Cardone, Grant. The 10X Rule®: The Only Difference Between Success and Failure. Hoboken: John Wiley & Sons, Inc., 2011.

Doyle, Robert J. Gainsharing and Productivity: A Guide to Planning, Implementation, and Development. New York: Amacom, 1983.

Duncan Mitchell, Geoffrey. A Hundred Years of Sociology. New Brunswick: Transaction Publishers, 1968.

Ericsson, A. and Robert Pool, Peak: How All of Us Can Achieve Extraordinary Things, London: Vintage, 2016.

Frost, Carl F., John H. Wakeley, and Robert A. Ruh, The Scanlon Plan for Organization Development: Identity, Participation and Equity. East Lansing: Michigan State University Press, 1974.

General Accounting Office, Productivity Sharing Programs: Can They Contribute to Productivity Improvement?, AFMD–81–22, March 3, 1981.

Goldratt, Eliyahu M. and Jeff Cox. The Goal: A Process of Ongoing Improvement. Croton-on-Hudson: North River Press, Inc., 1986.

Graham-Moore, Brian and Timothy L. Ross. Gainsharing: Plans for Improving Performance. Washington: BNA Books, 1990.

Grover, Tim S. and Shari Lesser Wenk. Winning: The Unforgiving Race to Greatness. New York: Scribner, 2021.

Lesieur, Fred G., ed., The Scanlon Plan: A Frontier in Labor-Management Cooperation. Cambridge, Mass.: The MIT Press, 1958.

Masternak, Robert. Gainsharing: A Team-Based Approach to Driving Organizational Change. Scottsdale: WorldatWork, 2003.

Moore, Brian E. and Timothy L. Ross, The Scanlon Way to Improved Productivity. New York: Wiley-Interscience, 1978.

Thor, Carl G. Gainsharing: Best Management Practices. Menlo Park: Crisp Publications, 1999.

ABOUT THE AUTHOR

DR. CHARLES (CHUCK) DEBETTIGNIES has more than 20 years experience in the design, implementation, and use of gainsharing systems. He has helped more than 300 corporations in the US and Europe develop their own gainsharing systems.

Nationally recognized as an authority on the subject, he has worked with both service and manufacturing companies of three to 1,600 employees to achieve lasting success with gainsharing.

Dr. Chuck is an author, public speaker, and seminar leader, and holds a Ph.D. in Industrial and Organizational Psychology.

He is the President of Gainsharing Inc., a business consulting firm specializing in gainsharing systems. It offers information, training, design, and implementation assistance.

Would You Do Me a Favor?

THANK YOU FOR READING MY BOOK!

If you found this book helpful, would you do something for me that will help others who are looking for this type of information?

Please take two minutes now to leave a helpful review on Amazon letting me know what you thought of the book. Just go to:

Gainsharing.com/review

Thanks so much!

www.ingramcontent.com/pod-product-compliance
Lightning Source LLC
Chambersburg PA
CBHW031857200326
41597CB00012B/445